A Note f
Director of European Operations

Welcome to the first edition of Kaplan Test Prep and Admissions' LNAT preparation book! We want you to perform at your very best on test day, and that is what this book will help you do.

Entry into the UK's top law departments is becoming ever more competitive, and this situation is not predicted to change soon. The number and quality of applicants is increasing every year. As a result, a number of the more selective law departments now require applicants to take the National Admissions Test for Law (LNAT) to help them distinguish between highly-qualified candidates and assess whether they have the skills needed to do well in a law degree programme.

Kaplan Test Prep and Admissions is the world leader in test preparation, and our books, software, courses and tutoring services are second to none. Kaplan was founded in the US in 1938, and in the UK we have helped thousands of students do better on university admissions tests since 1994.

Take full advantage of all the strategies, practice questions and tests, and on-line materials available through buying this book, to make sure that test day presents no surprises and is as stress-free as possible for you.

If after working through this book, you would like further help with your LNAT preparation, Kaplan Test Prep and Admissions also offers specialised preparation courses and tutoring at its London Centre and at secondary schools across the UK. See our website or contact us at the address below for more information.

During a successful career in law you will encounter many challenges, and that is probably one of the reasons you were attracted to this career in the first place. View the LNAT as one of these challenges, as well an opportunity for you to show law departments that you are committed and well-suited to a career in law. We are pleased to be able to work with you on achieving this goal.

Good luck on test day!

Kind regards,

Louise Cook
Director of European Operations
Kaplan Test Prep and Admissions

London Centre
3-5 Charing Cross Road
London WC2H 0HA
Tel: 020 7930 3130
Fax: 020 7930 8009
london_centre@kaplan.com
www.kaptest.com/uk

LNAT®

National Admissions Test for Law

by the Staff of Kaplan Test Prep and Admissions

KAPLAN
PUBLISHING
New York • Chicago

Contributing Editor: Darcy Galane
Editorial Director: Jennifer Farthing
Editor: Eileen McDonnell
Production Artist: David Chipps
Cover Designer: Carly Schnur

Published by Kaplan Publishing, a division of Kaplan, Inc.
888 Seventh Ave.
New York, NY 10106

Printed in the United States of America

June 2006
10 9 8 7 6 5 4 3 2

ISBN-13: 978-1-4195-4164-3
ISBN-10: 1-4195-4164-1

Kaplan Publishing books are available at special quantity discounts to use for sales promotions, employee premiums, or educational purposes. Please call our Special Sales Department to order or for more information at 800-621-9621, ext. 4444, email kaplanpubsales@kaplan.com, or write to Kaplan Publishing, 30 South Wacker Drive, Suite 2500, Chicago, IL 60606-7481.

Table of Contents

AVAILABLE ONLINE

Online Companion

The best preparation for a standardized test is practice in the test format. That's why we've provided even more practice in your online companion which can be accessed at **kaptest.com/LNATbooksonline**. Look there for additional reading passages and questions and more essay practice with a sample response.

Updates and Corrections

The material in this book is up-to-date at the time of publication. However, the LNAT Consortium Ltd may have instituted changes in the test after this book was published. Be sure to carefully read the materials you receive when you register for the test. If there are any important late-breaking developments—or any changes or corrections to the Kaplan test preparation materials in this book—we will post that information at **kaptest.com/publishing**.

Feedback and Comments

If you have comments or suggestions about this book, we invite you to fill out our online survey form at **kaplansurveys.com/books**. Your feedback is extremely helpful as we continue to develop high-quality resources to meet your needs.

Introduction: How to Use This Programme

The LNAT is probably a new testing experience for you. And Kaplan is a totally unique test preparation programme.

Kaplan has more experience preparing students for standardized tests than any other test prep programme. This book not only gives you the material you need to study for the LNAT, it will help you to learn *how* to study effectively for this particular test.

Clearly, you are a capable, bright student, and you may be thinking that of course you know how to study—after all you've been doing a good job of studying for years. But, standardized tests are different from other tests to which you may be accustomed, so the study methods are different too.

STANDARDIZED TESTS ARE DIFFERENT

Studying for a standardized test does not involve memorizing facts or demonstrating your knowledge of a particular body of knowledge. Because standardized tests are geared towards determining your aptitude for a type of intellectual work, studying prepares you to perform to the best of your ability. While some test makers contend that it is impossible to study for a standardized test, it has been clearly shown that practice makes a crucial difference in test takers' performance.

Consider for example, a physical test that is administered to determine a candidate's aptitude for firefighting. The exam does not test the candidates' skills at putting out fires or their knowledge of firefighters' equipment and procedures, but rather tests their strength and dexterity, the skills they will need to become successful firemen. While each person has a certain natural level of strength and coordination, both skills can certainly be developed and honed in such a way that a candidate could significantly alter his or her performance on such a physical exam. No one would dissuade a candidate from lifting weights or practicing running obstacle courses in preparation for the test.

Mental strength and dexterity can be exercised in much the same way, and the Kaplan method is designed to get you into top mental shape. To get the most from the Kaplan "work out" it is important to follow all the steps in the programme.

STEP ONE: READ CHAPTERS 1 AND 2

Chapter 1 introduces you to the LNAT. What is the test for? What is it like? How is it marked?

Chapter 2 gives you some general strategies for mastering the test and familiarizes you with the details of sitting for the LNAT.

These chapters lay the foundation for the test preparation programme.

STEP TWO: TAKE THE DIAGNOSTIC TEST

The diagnostic test appears in Part Two. Use this test to assess your strengths and weaknesses.

Addressing your weaknesses while acknowledging and bolstering your strengths will guide your study plan.

STEP THREE: TRY AN ONLINE ESSAY PROMPT

Your online companion includes a prompt similar to those you will see on test day.

1. Write a practice essay, allowing yourself 40 minutes and working under test-like conditions.
2. When you are finished, compare your esssay to the mode response provided.

STEP FOUR: CREATE A PERSONALIZED STUDY PLAN

Your plan will be determined by the amount of time available for you to prepare before your test date, and by your personal strengths and weaknesses.

Use a calendar or digital organizer to plan your study sessions. Each study session should be no more than three hours. These skills are best developed in regular, short sessions.

Be Realistic

Make a schedule that you can stick to; you will only undermine your confidence if you set an over-ambitious schedule and then fall behind. Allow yourself realistic time off for socialising and other activities.

Work Methodically

Chapter 3 is divided into three sections, each followed by a set of practice questions. You might plan to complete one section per study session. Your performance on these practice questions will indicate if you are making progress addressing your weaknesses. Depending on your progress you might need to adjust your practice schedule.

Devote at least a few sessions to the essay portion, even if you consider yourself a strong writer. Writing an essay in 40 minutes requires special focus and skills. Chapter 4 will be your starting point. Read the strategies before you attempt to complete any practice essays. You might plan to write one practice essay per study session.

Take Practice Tests

After you have completed chapters 3 and 4, take a practice test. This book includes a complete practice test, which you can take in one study session, and then review the multiple-choice answer explanations immediately, while it is still clear in your mind why you made the choices you did. Be sure to read the answer explanations very carefully and do a thorough analysis of your performance.

Again, you may need to reassess your study plan based on your practice test results. You might review the essay in your next session, when you can look at it with fresh eyes and evaluate how well you committed your ideas to paper.

Plan to take the online practice test offered on the official LNAT site at least one or two weeks before the actual test. Be sure to leave time to review your answers.

Access Our Online Companion

Practice online with two more reading passages and question sets available in your online companion, accessible through **kaptest.com/LNATbooksonline**. If you have more time in your schedule, you can practise the skills you learned in this book's exercises as you read articles in the publications suggested in chapter 2. Essentially any mainstream, serious newspaper or magazine will contain articles that you can read critically to further develop your skills. As you read, think about the types of questions that might be asked on the LNAT: learning to think like the test makers will further develop your testing skills.

For additional essay practice, write responses to statements of opinion found in your reading. Always practise essay writing within the time and word-count limits of the test—preferably on a computer and using only the word-processing tools that will be available on test day.

STEP FIVE: STICK WITH YOUR PLAN

Once you have created your study plan, follow it through. Your personal study plan is a work in progress. You should reassess your strengths regularly.

Be Flexible

Revise your study plan as you go. You might find you need to spend more time on a particular skill. For instance, the essay portion might give you more trouble than you anticipated. In this case, you might benefit from another study session or two to develop your essay writing skills.

It is important to stick to your schedule. That is, don't put off studying and plan to catch up later. Procrastinating will place you under pressure as your test date approaches—precisely the wrong thing to do. One of the main goals of a study plan is to methodically and reliably build your confidence and comfort level.

The Final Countdown

Finally, the last chapter of this book offers some constructive advice for the week before your test date. Read this chapter at least a week before your appointment to make the most of this advice.

At Kaplan, we are confident that if you follow the steps in this book you will get the best results on your LNAT exam. Thank you for choosing Kaplan to help you prepare for your test, and good luck!

| PART ONE |

The LNAT

Chapter 1: **Introduction to the LNAT**

- **LNAT Purpose**
- **LNAT Format**
- **LNAT Scoring**
- **LNAT Registration**
- **LNAT Checklist**

You have taken any number of tests in your school career. From the earliest spelling and maths tests to your A-levels, you have prepared and sat for exams. Why is the LNAT different?

Unlike other tests that teachers use to assess your ability to recall and apply information learned and discussed in the classroom, the LNAT is designed to test your abilities. For this reason, you will need a new approach to preparing for this test. First you need to understand all about the LNAT. With a clear understanding of the test's purpose, its structure, and how universities use the results, your preparation will be more meaningful and directed.

Clearly you understand that the LNAT is an exam used by universities to help assess candidates for their legal courses. And you may be aware that it is a multiple-choice "standardized" test with an essay section. What else is there to know?

LNAT PURPOSE

Its full name, the National Admissions Test for Law, tells you something about the test. It is a nationally administered test—every student takes the same LNAT exam. That is, the University of East Anglia does not have its own test that differs from the test administered by the University of Glasgow. The LNAT is run by a consortium of UK universities, and it allows these universities to rate your performance against all the other candidates interested in attending law courses in a given academic year. While it is just one element in the admissions process, and universities consider a variety of factors such as school performance and A-level results, the LNAT is an opportunity for you to distinguish yourself among your peers.

Even though the LNAT is called a "test for law", it does not ask any questions specifically related to the law. There are no facts to learn or lessons to review. The LNAT is designed to identify academic potential. In other words, do you have the intellectual skills necessary to make a successful law student?

You may be thinking, what is the point of studying? I either have the intellectual skills or I don't. And, in a way, you are right. You can't study for the LNAT the way you might for a geography test. But preparation can make a tremendous difference in your performance. Familiarizing yourself with the format of the test is the first step in being prepared.

LNAT FORMAT

The LNAT is an on-screen test with two sections: multiple choice and essay writing.

The first, multiple-choice portion includes 10 passages each followed by several questions. There are a total of 30 questions and you will have 80 minutes to complete the section. Unlike some standardized tests, the LNAT does not emphasize speed. The test developers have tried to allow a "reasonable" amount of time for candidates to consider their choices carefully. However, time is limited, so developing the right pace is an important aspect of your preparation.

The questions test verbal comprehension and reasoning skills, the skills that are necessary for law students. Each passage, ranging in length from about 400 to 600 words, is followed by questions that test understanding, interpretation, analysis, synthesis, induction, and deduction. There will be much more about mastering these questions later in the book.

The writing portion consists of five questions on a variety of topics from which you pick one. You will have 40 minutes to write a response to the question you have selected. An ideal LNAT essay is 500 to 600 words long, but your essay cannot exceed 750 words. Although it will be helpful to have a good grasp on everyday subjects, the purpose of the essay is to test your ability to select and organise ideas to put together a solid argument, and to assess your command of language.

LNAT SCORING

Your LNAT score is based solely on the multiple-choice portion of the test. You get one point for each correct answer on the 30 questions. No points are deducted for incorrect answers. A perfect score is 30. One wrong answer results in a score of 29, and so on.

Your essay is not scored; it is passed along unmarked to the universities to review as part of the selection process.

You will take the LNAT on a computer at a testing centre. Your test is marked automatically by computer and then passed along almost instantaneously to the universities to which you requested that your results be sent. You will select these universities when you register for the LNAT. You will also receive your score by post.

LNAT REGISTRATION

You register online at the official LNAT site, **www.lnat.ac.uk**. The site includes specific instructions about the registration process including a step-by-step guide. Here is an overview of the steps:

1. Create a web account with a user profile.

There are several screens that gather your personal information, such as email address, mailing address, phone, and so on. There is also a screen that asks you to select the universities to which you would like to send your results. You'll need to have considered this before you create your profile, and enter the information carefully. After all, a perfect LNAT score will only help you if it gets to the universities to which you are applying. (If you make a mistake you can update your profile prior to your test date.) After you have created your user profile, including a user name that you will use whenever you enter the system, you will get an email with a password that you will use to continue with your registration.

2. Book a test and pay.

Once you have a user name and password you can book your test. You have to pay when you make your booking. Within the UK, the LNAT costs 30 pounds, and outside the UK, 50 pounds. You can use a major credit card to pay online, but the LNAT does have a voucher system for people who do not have a major credit card. There is also a bursary scheme that waives the fee for students who receive certain state benefits. There are seven steps to booking a test, and each is carefully explained on the website.

Some important things to remember:

- You have to select the test you want to take. There are actually two versions of the LNAT: the regular sitting and the extended time. If you are entitled to extended time because of dyslexia or some other condition you can select the extended time test. Universities will check on entitlement.
- Some screens, such as "selecting the language for your test", are irrelevant. This is a generic Pearson VUE site, which includes options that are applicable to other tests.
- Selecting a test centre. You can search centres by geographic criteria such as city or postal code. Keep in mind that venues in city centres will be the busiest, so you might want to select a venue in an outskirts area to get a wider range of appointment times. You can search the test centre sites on the main website prior to booking your test, and it might be helpful to have already selected the centres where you can take the test before you get to the booking stage.
- Appointments. If the appointments at the test centre you selected are not satisfactory you can return to the test centre screen and choose another test centre. You can toggle back and forth until you get the optimal test centre and date.
- Review stage. You can change aspects of your user profile at this stage if necessary.
- Confirm stage. This screen includes important information about rescheduling your test. Be sure you read and understand this information.
- Receipt stage. After you have confirmed your order a receipt will be sent to the email address you provided for your user profile. You will need this receipt to check-in for your test. It should arrive in your in-box quite soon after you complete your registration.

3. Making changes to your profile or booking

You'll need your user name (created as part of your user profile) and your password (sent to you by email) to sign in. Once you are signed in you can edit your user profile by selecting either personal information (to change your email, phone number, and the like) or testing programs (to add your UCAS number or to change the list of universities where you are sending your results). You can also cancel or change your booking. However, there are some exceptions. You ***must*** change your booking at least two working days prior to your appointment. If you cancel for some reason prior to this deadline, your test fee will be fully refunded. The rescheduling process is very similar to the initial registration process and is clearly explained on the LNAT site.

LNAT CHECKLIST

Before You Start

- Visit the official LNAT site: **www.lnat.ac.uk**
- Find deadlines for your academic year
- Familiarize yourself with the registration process
- Complete UCAS (University and Colleges Admission Service) admissions form
- Receive your unique UCAS number

Register for the LNAT online

- When booking your test sitting, be sure to select an appointment that will give you enough time to prepare
- Receive confirmation email from Pearson VUE; check and report any errors immediately

Create A Test Prep Calendar

- Review "How to Use This Book"
- On a calendar or digital organizer, block out the weeks you have to prepare before you sit for the exam; be sure to plan some time off
- Revise your plan as necessary over the course of your preparation

Check Out Your Test Centre

- Make sure you know exactly how to get there and how long it takes
- Take a practice test on site, if possible, to familiarize yourself with the computer and screens

Test Day

- Bring Pearson confirmation email and acceptable ID
- Arrive at least 15 minutes before your appointment time to check in

Chapter 2: **Mastering the Test**

- **Taking the LNAT**
- **Multiple-Choice Section Strategies**
- **What to Expect on Test Day**
- **Preparation**
- **Stress Management**

By now you are familiar with the basics of the LNAT. You know what it is and why you are taking it. You are ready to master the test.

TAKING THE LNAT

There are several important factors that will affect your performance on the LNAT: your attitude, your confidence, and your comprehension of the test format.

Attitude

If you approach the LNAT with trepidation and see your impending appointment looming ominously before you, you have an attitude that will impede your success. If, on the other hand you view the LNAT as an opportunity and see yourself progressing confidently toward your test date, you have an attitude that will help your performance.

The key to developing the right attitude is to keep the test in proper perspective. Of course you take the test seriously. You have taken the trouble to buy this book to help you prepare. Chances are you will not fall into the trap of taking the test too lightly.

However, it is possible to take the test *too* seriously. Remember the LNAT is just one part of the admission process. How you fare on this test will *not* determine the rest of your life. Try to see the test as a challenge, one that you might even find enjoyable. The LNAT is an opportunity to match wits with not only your peers but also the test makers. Learning the skills to answer the LNAT questions with confidence can be very satisfying.

Preparation is the best way to ensure you can approach the test with a positive attitude. Preparing for the exam following the Kaplan method puts you ahead of many of your peers who will see the LNAT for the first time when they arrive at the test centre. Preparation breeds confidence.

Confidence

If preparation develops confidence, lack of preparation leads to self-doubt. And each state of mind feeds on itself. A confident test taker approaches a question calmly, reads all the options thoroughly, and chooses decisively. Having done so, the confident test taker attempts the next question with reinforced confidence. Confidence also allows you to take uncertainty in stride. If you find you are unable to answer a question with certainty, you will not become unravelled. You will be able to make an educated guess and move on to the next question.

On the other hand, a test taker who lacks confidence will have a difficult time making a decision, and this indecisiveness will breed anxiety and further erode confidence. Anxiety disrupts concentration, and soon the test becomes more of a struggle than a challenge.

How do you make sure you are a confident test taker? Adopting a positive attitude toward the test and preparing thoroughly will give you the confidence you need to conquer the LNAT.

Test Expertise

Nothing undermines confidence more than the unexpected. So, the more familiar you are with the test, the less likely it is that you will be surprised on test day. The diagnostic test, the practice questions, and the full-length practice test in this book will make you very familiar with the type of questions you will face.

You will also come to understand your own strengths and weaknesses. Of course, after you have finished your Kaplan preparation, you won't have real weaknesses, just questions that are more challenging for you than others. This understanding will help you move through the test with confidence. You might choose to pass over a particularly challenging question and move onto those that you find easier. This ability to identify your "easy" questions will help keep your confidence high as you move through the test.

There are two key factors in developing your test expertise: mastering multiple-choice strategies and being familiar with the mechanics of the test itself.

MULTIPLE-CHOICE SECTION STRATEGIES

Every question on the LNAT is worth one point. It doesn't matter if the answer is obvious or if you are completely flummoxed. You get one point if you get it right, and nothing if you leave it blank or get it wrong. These basic facts are the foundation of two crucial strategies: answering questions according to your ability and pacing.

Answer Questions According to Your Ability

Because the LNAT is a computer-based exam, you only see one question at a time. This can make it challenging to assess the relative difficulty of the questions. Unlike a paper test booklet, you cannot flip through the pages to get a sense of the test as a whole. Nonetheless, it is important to recognize that some question types will be more challenging to you than others.

The LNAT programme allows you to skip questions and to move back and forth between questions, making it possible to answer questions in the order of your ability not just in the order they appear in the test. Unlike some tests, the questions on the LNAT do not get more difficult as you move through the test, so if you waste time agonizing over one question, you might miss the opportunity to answer some questions that are easy for you at the end of the test. Because of time constraints it will be not make sense to preview all the questions to ascertain their difficulty before you answer them. However, you should skip over a question type that you typically get wrong to ensure that you have the opportunity to get through the entire test.

Answer Every Question

Because you don't lose any points for wrong answers it is a good idea to make a quick guess after you have scanned the answer choices before moving on. This way, if you run out of time, you have selected an answer that at least has a chance of being correct.

An especially effective strategy is to move around within the group of questions that relate to a particular passage. For example, the first question following a passage might be a type with which you have difficulty, but the second and third might be types that you always get right. If you answer the second and third questions first, you will have greater confidence when you attack the first question.

Ideally you should answer all the questions that relate to a passage before moving on, because the passage will be fresh in your mind. For example, if you skip a question that relates to the second passage and return to it at the end of the test, the chances are you will need to reread the passage to refresh your memory. This might cost you valuable time.

Use the Whiteboard Strategically

You will need to make a notation on your whiteboard of the number of any of the questions to which you want to return at the end of the test. The LNAT programme has a clever review screen that appears after you have reached the last question. This screen allows you to select the question numbers that you want to review. It also highlights any questions that you did not answer. The programme then takes you to the questions that you selected for review. The mechanics of this feature are explained in more detail below. The point here is that you need to keep track of the numbers of the questions that you want to review.

Develop Your Pacing

Even though the LNAT is not intended to test your ability to answer questions quickly, you still need to answer all 30 questions in 80 minutes. There are ten passages, which means you have roughly eight minutes to read each passage carefully and answer the two-to-four questions associated with each passage. It is not a cracking pace, but you can't afford to allow yourself to get bogged down on one passage or question.

Your goal is to get through all the questions in less than 80 minutes, allowing yourself some extra time to go back to those questions you marked for review.

However, you should not go too quickly. There is enough time to read the passages carefully and consider your answers in a calm, methodical way. Each screen on the LNAT gives you the elapsed time, so you do not need to constantly check your watch or rely on any other clock.

While it is important to be aware of the elapsed time, and your progress through the test, do not let the ticking clock make you nervous. Remain focused on the questions not the clock, and try to pick up your pace only when you see that you are not on track to complete all 30 questions.

How do you achieve this delicate balance of controlling your time, rather than being controlled by the clock? The answer, as you might guess, is practice. The more familiar you are with the test, and the more practised you are at answering LNAT questions, the easier you will find it to manage your time on test day.

WHAT TO EXPECT ON TEST DAY

Arrive *at least* 15 minutes early at your test centre, where the check-in agent will look at your identification and email confirmation.

You will be asked either to wait in the seating area until your test time or to proceed directly into the testing room, if your test time is imminent. You will be assigned a numbered desk and computer terminal, with a whiteboard and pen. There is an invigilator present in the test room, seated so as to see all the computer terminals. The computer runs only the LNAT programme and has no other functionality.

The first screen you will see explains the two sections of the test. Of course, you will be very familiar with the test by the time you arrive at the test centre. After you have scrolled through the information, you can move to the next screen, a non-disclosure agreement. After you have read the agreement you are asked if you are ready to begin. As soon as you select "yes," your test begins and time starts elapsing.

The Multiple-Choice Questions

For the multiple-choice section, the computer screen is divided into two panels. On the left is the passage, which will have a scroll bar if it is longer than a full screen, and on the right is one question with five answer options.

The computer only allows you to select one answer—reducing the chance of "user errors". When you have answered a question, you will click the "next" button to move to the next question. The upper right of the screen gives you the time *remaining* in your test in hours, minutes, and seconds. The lower right corner gives you the question number—for example, "item 5 of 30". There is also a "previous" button that allows you to return to the previous question.

Changing Your Answers: You can change the answer to any question at any point in the exam. However, before you get to the final review screen, you have to page through the questions in sequence to get to the question you want to change. This is why it is most efficient to move only between a group of questions related to a passage, answer all those questions, and then move on.

Going Back to Unanswered Questions: When you get to the last question and select "next" you will automatically go to the item review screen. This screen gives you several options. If you left any questions unanswered they will be highlighted in yellow. One option is to "review incomplete items", which will take you to the questions you left blank. You can move back and forth between these questions using the "previous" and "next" buttons. You will also have the option to "return to review screen" where you have two more options.

You can select questions for review by ticking a box next to the question number. (This is why it is important to note on your whiteboard the questions you want to review.) This will send you to the selected group of questions, and again you will be able to move back and forth among the selected questions using the "previous" and "next" buttons.

Review All: Your other option is "review all" which permits you to start at the first question and move through the questions in order. This option should not be necessary, as you should only have a handful of questions that require a second look.

When you have completed your review, you can return to the review screen and select "end review" to complete the multiple-choice section of the test. After you have selected "end review" the programme asks if you are sure you want to leave this portion of the test. If you select "yes," you will move on to the essay portion of the test.

The Essay

In the essay portion, you will see a new screen, quite similar to the message window in an email programme. The first screen has the first question; you can move to the next question by selecting "next". There are five screens in total. You will only write an essay for one of the questions.

Simply type your essay directly into the text box, as you would an email message. The programme includes cut, copy, and paste features, like most word processing programs, but no other features (so, no spell check for those of you who rely on the computer to correct spelling mistakes). The programme also has an automatic word count, shown in the lower left corner of the screen. The programme will not accept more than 750 words.

In this day and age, most of you will find the computer-based test format comfortable and similar to computer functions you use everyday. However, it is important to be aware of the limits and capabilities of the LNAT testing programme before you enter the test centre. You don't want any surprises on test day.

PREPARATION

The LNAT is a computer-based test. The more familiar and confident you are with the mechanics of the test, the better you will be able to focus all your energy and skills on answering the questions.

Practise reading on your computer screen. An important part of your preparation for the LNAT is reading papers and journals critically to develop your analytical reading skills. Read online journals and newspapers as much as possible so you will be comfortable reading passages on a computer screen in the test setting. Some good sites to visit include:

- www.economist.com
- www.guardian.co.uk
- http://news.bbc.co.uk
- www.the-tls.co.uk
- www.timesonline.co.uk

Develop an economical notation method so you can make notes and plan your essay efficiently. You will not be able to bring any scrap paper into the exam with you; rather, you will be provided with an erasable whiteboard which you will use to make notes as you read the passages, but there will be a limited amount of space. A consistent notation system that you have practiced using while reading online articles, planning practice essays, or taking the practice tests will help you use the whiteboard to your advantage during the test.

When you take your practice test, try to replicate the test conditions. You are not allowed any personal items in your test cubicle. This means, in addition to no pens or paper of your own, no water, sweets, coffee, or tea.

Visit the official LNAT site to take an online practice test. Not only will this give you more practice questions, in addition to those provided in this book, but you will also have a chance to move through the computer screens before you sit for the real exam. You can also tour a test centre—a great way to eliminate another uncertainty.

STRESS MANAGEMENT

With the right attitude, a well-developed confidence, and familiarity with the test environment, you've eliminated most of the major causes of anxiety among test takers. Common sources of anxiety are: placing too much importance on the test, lack of confidence in one's ability, negative thinking and the unexpected. However, it won't do you any harm to be aware of some stress management techniques to handle a sudden bout of test taker anxiety.

First, remember that some stress is good. The right amount of adrenaline will give you energy and focus. So, if you feel a little keyed-up as you enter the test centre, you are probably in the right frame of mind.

However, too much stress can have the opposite effect, destroying concentration and sapping energy. Some people are more prone to test taker anxiety than others. If you know that tests make you anxious, practice is one of your best weapons to combat stress. But it is important to practise in a way that boosts your confidence.

Set Realistic Goals

Review the "How to Use this Book" section and outline a reasonable study plan. Never plan to practise for more than three hours at a time. And give yourself time for breaks. Setting an unrealistic study plan will only cause anxiety and erode your confidence.

Focus on Your Strengths

In the next section you will take a diagnostic test. The test will help you identify your strengths and weaknesses. Do *not* use the diagnostic test to confirm your worst fears or reinforce any feelings of inadequacy. Make a list of your strengths. Think of these strengths as fuel you will use during the exam. As you practice and eliminate any "weaknesses" you identify, you will be adding to your "fuel tank."

Imagine Yourself Succeeding

Close your eyes and imagine yourself in a relaxing situation. Breathe easily and naturally, and think of a real-life situation in which you did well on a test or did well on an assignment. Focus on this success. Now, turn your thoughts to the LNAT and associate that feeling of success with the upcoming exam. Simply imagine yourself taking the LNAT with this feeling of confidence and relaxed control. If you feel anxiety creeping up while you are taking the actual test, follow these same steps to regain your sense of confident control.

Exercise

During your study schedule, physical exercise, even a short, brisk walk, stimulates your mind and body and improves your ability to concentrate. Make time in your schedule for some regular exercise.

Eat Well

Good nutrition helps you focus and think clearly. Eat plenty of fruit and vegetables; low-fat protein such as fish, chicken, and beans; and whole grains such as wholewheat bread, brown rice, and pasta. Avoid sweets and fatty and salty foods, which only give you a short-lived burst of energy and ultimately make you feel more tired. Too much caffeine can make you nervous and interfere with your concentration.

Take a Deep Breath

Slow, deep breaths are a simple way to get stress under control. If you become anxious during study or during the test, take a moment to inhale deeply, consciously filling your lungs, and then slowly exhale. Do this a few times until your body (especially your neck and shoulders) is relaxed and your mind is calm and focused.

Stretch

A good stretch is another way to regain your composure. If your attention starts to wander when you are studying, standing up to stretch and get your blood flowing can help bring your mind back into focus. During the test, stretching your arms and back can help you relax if you feel yourself becoming stressed.

| PART TWO |

Diagnostic

Diagnostic Test

In order to best use this programme, you must first understand where your current strengths and weaknesses lie. Your results in answering the questions in this diagnostic test will assist you in developing a study plan.

Allow yourself 40 minutes to complete the following test, which includes the types of questions you will encounter on the LNAT. It contains 15 questions, rather than the usual 30. To make it an effective measure of how you might perform if you were to take the LNAT today, take the test in one sitting and under conditions as test-like as possible.

When you have completed the test, check your answers against the answer key to determine your score. Then carefully read the answer explanations, not only for those you got wrong but also for those you got right. Even if you answered a question correctly, the answer explanation may include helpful hints about that particular question type. You want to make sure that you used sound reasoning to select the answer—in case you just made a lucky guess, and you want to know that you reached your answer in the surest and most efficient way possible.

DIAGNOSTIC TEST: NATIONAL ADMISSIONS TEST FOR LAW

This half-length multiple-choice test has 5 subsections, each having between 2 and 4 questions. Answer all 15 questions, selecting only one of the possible answers listed for each question.

Time: 40 minutes

I Turkey and the EU

Members of the European Union concur that a shared future is the way forward, but not all members see Turkey as a part of that future. According to *The Observer UK,* if European Foreign Ministers can agree upon a common negotiating position in emergency meetings called upon recently, the EU will start talks about admitting Turkey to the inner sanctum. Yet although every EU member-state bar Austria, whose objections prompted the meetings, officially endorses Turkey's candidacy, no single country can muster a majority for entry in opinion polls. The Continent's electorates, including those in the UK, don't regard Turkey as European.

This does not make it right to block Turkey's application. As Lord Patten, a former EU commissioner, warned yesterday, such xenophobia reveals a failure of leadership which can only seriously damage the West's relations with Islam. There is a strong case for entry which governments must now start making. Europe needs Turkey as a custodian of prosperity and democracy and an exemplar and anchor for all the countries that surround it. It needs Turkish labor, and the Turkish guarantee of oil and gas from central Asia. Above all, it needs to send a positive message to the 12 million Muslims who already live within Europe.

During the past decade, Turkey has moved heaven and earth to meet the EU accession criteria, and it now presents itself as a democratic state and a market economy governed by the rule of law. True, there remains a culture war in Turkey between those who incline to secularism, and those who incline to fundamentalism. True, too, that one of Turkey's leading novelists, Orahan Pamuk, awaits trial in December for raising the subject of the murder of Armenians during the Great War. Human-rights abuses are routinely reported, and free discussion remains precarious. Such issues should be on the table for debate on Monday. But the way forward, for Turkey and for Europe, is to maintain the ambition of a shared future.

Source: *The Observer,* October 2005

1. Which of the following may be **inferred** from the passage?

    (a) Disagreement among rival social factions in Turkey may prevent its EU membership.

    (b) Turkey does not have a strong economy, which EU members consider a prerequisite for membership.

    (c) Turkey has large reserves of natural resources deemed vital to Western economic prosperity.

    (d) The majority of Europeans welcome Turkey's membership in the EU.

    (e) The majority of Turkish citizens would welcome membership in the EU.

2. Which of the following is **not** stated in the passage?

    (a) Common ground must be found among EU member states before talks on admitting Turkey can begin.

    (b) Most Europeans do not consider Turkey to be a European nation.

    (c) Turkish citizens who live and work in European states would welcome Turkey's admittance to the EU.

    (d) The Turkish government at times arrests and detains citizens critical of its laws and policies.

    (e) Turkey has most of the economic and social hallmarks of a modern Western state.

II Naming Patterns

What will the next Atlantic hurricane be called? The World Meteorological Organization has run out of names for hurricanes this year, the first time since the current convention was adopted. With more than a month left to go for hurricane season, there have been 21 named storms in the Atlantic Ocean this year, and officials are planning to haul the contingency plan—using the letters of the Greek alphabet—out of storage, says a recent report from the Guardian UK.

As there can be 100 or so storms a year, meteorologists need a means of identifying individual storms to avoid confusion, especially as one or more storms may be followed and charted by many meteorologists simultaneously.

Early naming strategies were informal and individualistic in their approach. For several hundred years in the Caribbean, hurricanes were named after the saint's day on which they occurred. For example, 'Hurricane San Felipe' struck Puerto Rico on 13 September 1876. Later, latitude and longitude were used, but this was found to be complicated and prone to error. According to one report, the first use of a proper name for a tropical storm was by an Australian forecaster in the early part of the last century who reputedly named his storms after politicians he didn't like. Maybe that's an approach that deserves a comeback!

The BBC states that by 1950 the first formal name strategy was in place for North American cyclones. The storms took their names from the phonetic alphabet of the time—*Able*, *Baker*, *Charlie*, etc—and this continued until 1952. By the following year, the US Weather Bureau decided to switch to female first names, and then decided to finally include male first names in the list in 1979. There is currently a list of 21 names used in rotation, with the names alternating between male and female. The letters *Q*, *U*, *X*, *Y*, and *Z* are not used, because few names begin with those letters.

The naming of cyclones today continues much in the same vein. Each basin or region has an agreed list of names, with the first cyclones in the Atlantic basin and in the eastern Pacific region each year given an A name. The year's first cyclone in the central Pacific region takes the next name on the list, regardless of which letter it starts with. Of course, if a storm should wander from one basin into another, it will be rewarded with a new name from that region. There's no wonder some of these storms are angry—they could have huge identity crises.

Source: "What Will the Next Atlantic Hurricane Be Called?"

The Guardian, October 22 2005

3. What is the **main** point of this passage?

   (a) Hurricanes are unpredictable and destructive forces of nature.

   (b) There are many different systems used around the world for the naming of hurricanes.

   (c) Hurricane names are based on a standardized system of male and female names.

   (d) Hurricanes are named differently, depending upon the regions in which they appear.

   (e) The naming of hurricanes is futile, given that there are now so many of them.

4. With which of the following would the author of the passage be **most** likely to agree?

   (a) The US Weather Bureau should not be solely in charge of naming hurricanes.

   (b) Using both male and female names for identifying hurricanes is a confusing strategy.

   (c) There's no predicting how hurricanes will behave, even if we name them to track their progress.

   (d) The current system used to identify and track hurricanes is a simple, elegant, and effective one.

   (e) A new hurricane naming system is needed because of their rising frequency and severity.

III Hobbes's Choice

In his book *Leviathan*, the seventeenth-century English philosopher Thomas Hobbes set out his doctrine of *modern natural rights* as the foundation of societies and legitimate governments. In the natural condition of mankind, while some men may be stronger or more intelligent than others, none are so strong and smart as to be beyond a fear of violent death. When threatened with death, man in his natural state cannot help but defend himself in any way possible. Self-defense against violent death is Hobbes' highest human necessity, and rights are born of necessity. In the state of nature, then, each of us has a right to everything in the world. Due to the scarcity of all things in the world, there is a constant, and rights-based, war of all against all. Life in the state of nature is "solitary, poor, nasty, brutish, and short".

But war isn't in man's best interest. According to Hobbes, man has a self-interested and materialistic desire to end war—"the passions that incline men to peace are fear of death, desire of such things are necessary to commodious living, and a hope by their industry to obtain them." He forms peaceful societies by entering into a social contract. Hobbes suggests that society is a population beneath an authority, to whom all individuals in that society surrender just enough of their natural right for the authority to be able to ensure internal peace and a common defense. This sovereign, whether monarchy, aristocracy, or democracy, should be *Leviathan*, an absolute authority. Law, for Hobbes, is the enforcement of contracts. The political theory of *Leviathan* varies little from that set out in the philosopher's two earlier works, *The Elements of Law* and *De Cive (On The Citizen)*.

Hobbes's state is infinitely authoritative in matters pertaining to aggression, one man waging war on another, or any matters pertaining to cohesiveness of the state. It can say nothing about what any man does otherwise—so long as one man does no harm to another, the sovereign should keep its hands off him. However, since there is no power above the sovereign, there is nothing to prevent the sovereign from breaking this rule. A sovereign also maintains equality with the state, since the common people would be "washed out" in the glare of their sovereign, which he likens to stars in the face of the sun. In essence, Hobbes' political doctrine is to do no harm. His negative version of the Biblical wisdom, in essence, reads: "Do not that to another, which thou wouldst not have done to thyself." This is contrasted with the Christian Golden Rule, which encourages actively doing unto other. This teaching, for Hobbes, leads to nothing but social chaos.

Leviathan was written during the English Civil War. Much of the book is occupied with demonstrating the necessity of a strong central authority to avoid the evil of discord and social strife. Any abuses of power by this authority are to be accepted as the price of peace. In particular, the doctrine of separation of powers is rejected, as the sovereign must retain control of civil, military, judicial, and ecclesiastical order. Hobbes explicitly states that the sovereign has the authority to assert control over matters of faith and doctrine, and that not to do so is a recipe for disaster. Hobbes presents his own religious theory, but states that he would defer to the will of the sovereign as to whether his theory was acceptable. It is argued by Hobbes' detractors that his view further marks Hobbes as a supporter of the religious policy of the post-Civil War English republic, that of *independency*.

Today, the adjective *Hobbesian* is sometimes used in modern English to refer to a situation characterized by unrestrained, selfish, and uncivilized competition. This usage, now well-established, is unfortunate for two reasons. First of all, Hobbes' book *Leviathan* describes such a situation, but only in order to criticize it; secondly, Thomas Hobbes himself was a rather timid and bookish person. Other uses, which gained in popularity immediately after Hobbes published his book, carry connotations of atheism, and of the belief that "might makes right".

5. What is the author's **main** point in this passage?

   (a) Thomas Hobbes's *Leviathan* discards the values of democracy in favour of a monarchy with strong centralized authority.

   (b) *Leviathan* describes a social reality where the natural rights of citizens prevail over any sort of powerful state.

   (c) *Leviathan* proposes that citizens must cede a portion of their power to a governing entity which guarantees the autonomy of the citizens' natural rights.

   (d) Thomas Hobbes was a selfish atheist who believed that the natural order of things could be simply stated as "every man for himself".

   (e) Thomas Hobbes was an influential thinker in his day, but his beliefs have largely passed out of fashion.

6. Which of the following can be **inferred** from the passage?

   (a) The governing principles in *Leviathan* could be construed as authoritarian, and seized upon by a despotic ruler wishing 'peace' for the populace.

   (b) *Leviathan* was adopted by colonial rebels as one of their key philosophical texts during the American Revolution.

   (c) Hobbes feared that common people were incapable of governing their own affairs, and his disgust with this realization led him to write his book.

   (d) Hobbes believed that kings had a divine right to rule over their subjects, and that supreme power should rest with the monarch.

   (e) Hobbes distrusted any form of strong central authority, and thought that power should be evenly held by different governing members of the state.

7. Which of the following is **not** stated in the passage?

   (a) Hobbes believed that everyday life in the seventeeth century was not particularly satisfying by modern standards.

   (b) The modern democratic ideal of checks and balances was not a premise Hobbes thought justified.

   (c) The lessons of the Biblical parable "Do unto others" were dismissed by Hobbes as an exemplary bit of social wisdom.

   (d) Extensive and intricate systems of taxation were necessary to maintain social stability in seventeenth-century England.

   (e) Matters of religion must necessarily defer to the wishes of the sovereign, since to do otherwise would lead to strife and discord.

IV. New York Art

Abstract Expressionism was the first truly modern movement in American painting, and established the nation's cultural identity in the years immediately following the Second World War. Contemporaneous developments in jazz, fiction, and poetry helped shift the world's attention to New York City, supplanting Paris as a tastemaking capital. It's appropriate, then, that members of this movement are sometimes collectively referred to as the New York School.

Abstract Expressionist paintings do not exhibit a homogeneous look. The paintings produced by these American artists are as varied and singular as those who made them. This label was coined in 1946 by the critic Robert Coates. A host of other critics, chief among them Clement Greenberg, would soon follow in championing the work. Generally speaking, 'AbEx' paintings have several traits in common. Foremost among these is the artists' preference for working on a massive scale. Artists such as Jackson Pollock, Clyfford Still, Mark Rothko, and Barnett Newman all made large paintings that would not hang comfortably on the walls of the average Park Avenue apartment. Another characteristic of these various paintings is an emphasis on the flatness of their support. This is done through a compositional strategy that came to be understood as an 'allover' approach. This method abolished a hierarchical organization of the painting in favor of a non-illusionistic, even distribution of elements across its surface.

The most notorious of the AbEx painters was Jackson Pollock. He was born and raised in the American West, and the myth of his rugged individualism typifies the cult of personality that these artists and their critics cultivated around their work. His terrific drip paintings, with their tangled skeins of silver, black, white, violet, and teal paint poured directly onto the creamy tan canvas, evoke tremendous shimmering vistas. It was widely agreed these works were technically accomplished masterpieces of brute materialism tempered by an elegant lyricism, and were the peer of anything produced before the War by artists such as Pablo Picasso and Henri Matisse.

Clyfford Still and Mark Rothko both became known for presenting vast areas of intense, subtly inflected color in their oversized canvases. Still's paintings are energized by raw, flamelike shapes of thick impasto, the colors severe, saturated, and contrasting in value. Rothko organized his works differently, choosing instead to present just two or three rectangles of luminous color floating in an atmospheric space. Both artists were deeply invested in the emotional states they wished their work to convey, and frequently found themselves in conflict with both their fellows and their public.

Barnett Newman was a native-born New Yorker, who came to a mature understanding of his painting rather late in life. Newman was nonetheless one of the most important figures of his generation. His vision was instrumental in inspiring a younger generation of artists to pursue ideas that would eventually come to be known as Minimalism. Newman discarded the usual narrative and pictorial content of previous painting, since he understood quite simply that an actual experience of color and shape was sufficient to provoke a complex emotional response. Many of his canvases approach dimensions of ten, twelve, or fourteen feet on a side, are covered in brilliant hues like scarlet, indigo, or aqua, and are delineated by differing bands of color the artist dubbed 'zips'. It was Newman's enduring achievement as an artist to devise a method of painting that activated space as an entity, thus drawing time into its embrace.

Abstract Expressionism, for the most part, ceased being innovative after the efforts of its main proponents were accepted as legitimate. A second generation of gestural painters who followed Pollock, Still, Rothko, Newman were widely seen as imitative and academic. For those who prided themselves on grit, resourcefulness, and the romance of the studio, the inauthentic and the contrived were anathema. The movement was largely spent by the early 1960's, although its rigor and toughness inspired both Minimalism and Pop Art. As a style, though, Abstract Expressionism effectively challenged conventional European standards of taste and beauty. It conveyed the creative vitality of people living and working in a great metropolis after the end of a vicious period of global strife and destruction, constrained by nothing but the limits of their imaginations.

8. What could be considered the **main** point of the passage?

   (a) Modern art in post-World War II America was unpopular with the public at large

   (b) American modern art after the War was not as important as the work done in Europe before the War.

   (c) Modern American artists were isolated figures whose personality quirks limited the appeal of their work.

   (d) Abstract Expressionism was a short-lived artistic movement whose influence and popularity was limited.

   (e) The New York School helped create a strong cultural identity for America in the years immediately after World War II.

9. Which of the following could be **inferred** from the passage?

   (a) Jackson Pollock's fame grew because the romantic myth of his tough cowboy personality seemed to suit his big paintings.

   (b) Abstract Expressionist paintings were usually not as technically accomplished as paintings by Matisse or Picasso and were not as popular with collectors.

   (c) The similar compositional strategies used by AbEx painters made most of their works indistinguishable from one another.

   (d) Although many artists lived in New York after World War II, Paris continued to be the leading modern tastemaker of the time.

   (e) Mark Rothko made very large paintings because surplus paint and canvas were inexpensive right after World War II.

10. Which of the following is **clearly** stated in the passage?

    (a) Abstract Expressionist paintings gained popularity because they were generally less expensive than modern European paintings.

    (b) Clyfford Still detested Mark Rothko, thinking Rothko had stolen many of his best ideas.

    (c) Barnett Newman always painted very quickly, using bright, simple colors, as he thought they conveyed his feelings most accurately.

    (d) One of Jackson Pollock's innovations was to pour paint directly on the surface of a blank canvas to which no colour had previously been applied.

    (e) Clyfford Still was jealous of the 'overnight success' that Jackson Pollock attained at a relatively early age.

11. Which of the following is **clearly** stated in the passage?

    (a) Clyfford Still would often withdraw his work from exhibitions if he felt the circumstances were less than optimum.

    (b) Mark Rothko sought to achieve a densely coloured, claustrophobic space in his paintings.

    (c) The Abstract Expressionist painters had strong critical supporters who were advocates of their work.

    (d) Jackson Pollock's work had a profound impact on his colleagues, and his work influenced a number of younger painters after his death.

    (e) The painters who followed in the footsteps of the New York School were far more successful in their endeavours.

12. Which of the following is **not** clearly stated in the passage?

    (a) Abstract Expressionist paintings are clearly the work of individual artists with distinct subjective styles.

    (b) Abstract Expressionists created a unique compositional approach to picture making which differed from their European counterparts.

    (c) Abstract Expressionist paintings were judged by a set of aesthetic standards that had much in common with previous painting styles.

    (d) Abstract Expressionist paintings were largely rejected by both critics and the public during the time of their production.

    (e) The New York School had an impact on its unique historical moment, but left no lasting artistic legacy.

V Dark Beer

Stout is a type of dark beer that is made using either roasted malts or roasted barley. It was originally a variant of porter beer, which was first recorded as being made and sold in London in the eighteenth century, and subsequently became widely popular in Great Britain and Ireland. The earlier meaning of the adjective 'stout' was 'proud' or 'brave', but after the fourteenth century it was ascribed the meaning 'strong'. The first use of the word in connection with beer was attached to the *Stout-Porter* brewed in 1820 in Ireland although it had been brewing traditional porters since 1759. 'Stout' still meant 'strong', however, so it was related to any kind of beer, as long as the beer was, indeed, strong. In the UK, for example, it was possible to find something called 'stout pale ale', which did not resemble a porter or a true stout in any way save that it was a fermented beverage. It was only later that the term 'stout' became associated exclusively with porter, and became a catch-all synonym for dark beer.

Stout differs from porter in being darker and richer. It achieves these qualities through the use of more roasted malt. Stout also has a higher alcoholic content. Consequently, the beers are considered distinct, although sometimes it is difficult to distinguish them. Generally speaking, stouts can be placed into two main categories, sweet and bitter. There are several kinds of each. Irish stout, also called dry stout, is the original product. It is very dark in colour and often has a toasted, coffee-like taste. Imperial stout was originally brewed in England for export to the court of the Russian Tsar. It is highly hopped, very dark, and has a very high alcohol content. Milk stout, sometimes referred to as sweet or cream stout, possesses an increased sweetness due to the addition of lactose before fermentation. Oatmeal stout, as the name suggests, has oats added to it during the brewing process, which makes the resulting beer even sweeter and smoother than milk stout. Chocolate and espresso stouts both typically use the darkest roasted malts, resulting in the darkest and occasionally most bitter of all stouts. Sometimes real chocolate or coffee are added to these brews, but this is usually seen as a bit of a gimmick and is abhorred by purists.

During the end of the nineteenth century, it was commonly believed that stout was a beneficial, healthy drink, with a reputation for increasing strength and stamina in the drinker. As such, it was widely drunk by athletes and by nursing women; doctors often prescribed it to aid in recovery from a variety of maladies. Stout does possess significant quantities of bioflavonoids and antioxidants, which may give it negligible health benefits. Today, stout is still brewed throughout Great Britain and Ireland, with English stout generally being sweeter than its Irish counterpart. Current or former nations of the British Commonwealth can each have their own local interpretations of the style. Stout is also available from breweries throughout the New World, from British Columbia and Quebec to Brooklyn and Jamaica.

13. What is the **main** point of the passage?

    (a) Stout and porter are interchangeable names for a single type of beer.

    (b) Stout is a specific type of beer, distinguishable from porter by its ingredients and brewing.

    (c) Only dark beers are generally known as stout.

    (d) All beer is called stout as long as it has a high alcohol content.

    (e) Stout is an exclusively English beer, although it has been copied by brewers in other countries.

14. Which of the following is **not** stated in the passage?

    (a) Stout is distinguished from porter by its darker colour and richer flavour.

    (b) The key ingredient in the production of stout is roasted malt.

    (c) Stout is a dark beer which may be sweet or bitter in flavour, and sometimes has a dry taste.

    (d) Both sweet and bitter varieties of stout are still made in various countries around the world.

    (e) Stout was named for drinkers who favoured the beer—rather portly, or 'stout', athletes, nursing mothers, and doctors.

15. Which of the following is **clearly** stated in the passage?

    (a) Although the first stout was brewed in Great Britain, is is now made throughout Europe and North America.

    (b) Stout is brewed using roasted malts and then stored in walnut barrels, which give it its dark colour.

    (c) Drinkers sometimes prefer darker, more flavourful stouts that are brewed with real chocolate or espresso.

    (d) Stout may be a dark, flavourful beer which initially tastes sweet on the palate, but has a dry or bitter finish.

    (e) Stout or strong porter beers were first available in London, but the first true stout was Irish in its origin.

ANSWERS AND EXPLANATIONS

Answer Key

1. (a)	9. (a)
2. (c)	10. (d)
3. (c)	11. (c)
4. (d)	12. (d)
5. (c)	13. (b)
6. (a)	14. (e)
7. (d)	15. (e)
8. (e)	

1. (a)

This is an *inference* question, as you must look for an answer that *must be true but is not explicitly stated* in the text; **(a)** is correct because unresolved cultural issues in Turkey, based on differences between secularism and fundamentalism, democracy and authoritarianism, pose unsettling questions for EU member nations.

(b) is incorrect because although it is stated that Turkey has a modern market economy, no indication is given as to its strength relative to EU member nations.

(c) is incorrect because no mention is made of Turkey's own natural resources; only those of its geographic neighbours are alluded to, albeit indirectly.

(d) and **(e)** are incorrect because little is made of the opinions of either the European or Turkish general populations regarding Turkey's proposed EU membership.

2. (c)

Remember that in this question, the correct answer *must not explicitly appear* in the text; **(c)** is correct since, although the text mentions that 12 million Muslims live in Europe, no mention is made of their ancestry—they are most certainly not all Turkish, nor are all Turkish immigrants Muslim—nor of their opinions on EU membership.

(a) The first paragraph of the text mentions consensus among EU nations related to talks concerning Turkey's proposed membership.

(b) The general populations of EU nations do not consider Turkey to be a European nation, as stated in the first paragraph.

(d) The Turkish author Orahan Parmuk was arrested and detained by the state for expressing his views on the Armenian genocide during WWI.

(e) The last paragraph calls attention to democratic processes and a market economy as features of the modern Turkish state.

3. **(c)**

This question asks the purpose or theme of the passage. The first sentence of the first paragraph asks, "What will the next Atlantic hurricane be called?", and the passage goes on to explain how the contemporary system used to name hurricanes was developed. Choice **(c)** is thus correct.

(a) makes a statement that is unsupported in the passage.

(b) contradicts the fact that the naming of hurricanes has been standardized since 1979.

(d) contradicts the logical naming of hurricanes based on the timing and the region in which they appear.

(e) is not supported by the passage and is an incorrect inference.

4. **(d)**

The passage explains the contemporary system in place for identifying and tracking hurricanes, including the contingency plan in use due to the unusual frequency of hurricanes this year. No other system is suggested to replace the current one. So **(d)** is therefore correct.

(a) is incorrect, as the author makes no suggestions as to who should be responsible for the naming of hurricanes.

(b) is incorrect, as the author makes no criticism of the methods used by meteorologists in naming the storms they track.

(c) is incorrect, as the author makes no statements on the unpredictability of hurricanes.

(e) is incorrect, as the author suggests no new system to replace the current one now in use.

5. **(c)**

Thomas Hobbes' *Leviathan* proposes that the natural rights of man form the basis of a social contract entered into with a supreme governing entity, be it a monarch, a class of aristocrats, or a democratic electorate, so **(c)** is correct.

(a) is incorrect; Hobbes advocates that no social system is inherently superior to another, as long as citizens' rights are protected by the governing sovereign.

(b) is incorrect; Hobbes insists that a social contract be instituted between the populace and its governing body, where neither prevail over the other.

(d) is incorrect; Hobbes maintains that citizens build peaceful communities of mutual self-interest based on a shared social contract.

(e) is incorrect; *Leviathan* remains an important and influential book to this day, presenting a model of a civil society based on individual rights and the limits of state power.

6. (a)

Hobbes places supreme authority in the hands of a monarchy or other form of power. It could therefore transpire that an unscrupulous sovereign would seek expansion of such power to maintain absolute control over the populace, and against their wishes, since there is not a governing body in place to counter such desire. One could therefore *infer* **(a)**.

(b) is incorrect, as no mention is made in the passage of social or political events which transpire outside of seventeeth-century England, and such an inference could easily be based on conjecture, without basis in fact.

(c) is incorrect, as *Leviathan* clearly states that people willingly relinquish some of their self-interest to enter into a social contract with the state.

(d) is incorrect, as Hobbes expresses no views concerning the divinity of rulers over those they rule.

(e) is incorrect, as Hobbes strongly believes in the autonomy of a strong central authority, which in his book he names *Leviathan.*

7. (d)

The passage makes no mention of how Hobbes thought the state should address matters of revenue, or how the populace should be expected to submit to such demands. Therefore, **(d)** is correct, as these questions are not addressed in the passage.

(a) is incorrect, as Hobbes states in his book that life for the common people was "solitary, poor, nasty, brutish, and short."

(b) is incorrect, as *Leviathan* quite explicitly rejects the doctrine of a separation of powers.

(c) is incorrect, as Hobbes believed that adherence to the letter of the Golden Rule would lead to complete social chaos.

(e) is incorrect, as Hobbes states that matters of belief must be subject to decisions deemed acceptable to the sovereign, lest questions of belief disturb the interests of civil society.

8. (e)

As members of the New York School, Abstract Expressionist painters created a truly modern American movement in the late 1940s, so **(e)** is correct.

(a) is incorrect, as modern art became increasingly popular in America in the years immediately following the war.

(b) is incorrect, as innovations in American painting after the war were increasingly seen as the peer of its European counterpart.

(c) is incorrect, as the cult of personality that the American artists cultivated around their work was of great importance.

(d) is incorrect, as movements including Minimalism and Pop Art took their inspiration from the legacy built by the New York School.

9. (a)

Jackson Pollock spent his boyhood amongst cowboys and native Americans, and these stories added to the myth of his creative personality. It could therefore be gathered that choice **(a)** is correct.

(b) is incorrect, as many 'AbEx' works, including Jackson Pollock's drip paintings, were virtuoso feats of painterly accomplishment.

(c) is incorrect, as the passage clearly states that the paintings made by the 'AbEx' artists were as varied as those who made them.

(d) is incorrect, as the first paragraph explains that the world's creative attention shifted from Paris to New York City immediately following WWII.

(e) is incorrect, as the paragraph makes no mention of the economic circumstances artists contended with after WWII had ended.

10. (d)

One of Jackson Pollock's great innovations consisted of pouring or dripping liquid paint directly onto raw canvas. The resulting webs of colour shimmered in ways similar to effects of light in a landscape. Therefore **(d)** is correct.

(a) is incorrect, as no mention is made of the relative value of American and European paintings.

(b) is incorrect, as the passage does not suggest any professional jealousies existing specifically between the two artists.

(c) is incorrect, as nothing is noted to the effect that Newman preferred one colour to the next in respect to his subjective feelings.

(e) is incorrect, as the passage clearly does not describe professional jealousies among members of the New York School.

11. (c)

This point is made in the second and third paragraphs; **(c)** is correct.

(a) is incorrect, as no mention is made of Still's exhibition history.

(b) is incorrect, as the passage states Rothko's paintings are atmospheric, the opposite of claustrophobic.

(d) is incorrect, as no mention is made of Pollock's immediate influence on his followers.

(e) is incorrect, since the gestural painters who followed the charter members of the New York School were often seen as less successful than original artists.

12. (d)

Abstract Expressionist artists had a number of critical champions, among them Robert Coates and Clement Greenberg. This is clearly stated in the second paragraph, so **(d)** is correct.

(a) is incorrect, as the passage describes the work of several artists with distinct individual styles.

(b) is incorrect, as the passage describes the "allover" compositional approach developed and favoured by the American artists.

(c) is incorrect, as the passage states that Abstract Expressionist painting effectively challenged conventional notions of beauty and taste.

(e) is incorrect, as the passage refers to the Minimalists and Pop artists who took the example of the New York School to heart, without imitating its stylistic conventions.

13. (b)

Stout is a specific type of dark beer made with roasted malts or barley, and is sometimes brewed with added ingredients such as oats or lactose, which distinguish it from other beers such as porter. Therefore, **(b)** is correct.

(a) is incorrect, as stout is distinguished from porter by the specific ingredients from which it is brewed.

(c) is incorrect, as beers high in alcohol that may have been light in colour, such as pale ale, were once referred to as 'stout' or strong.

(d) is incorrect, since although 'stout' did once mean 'strong,' it now commonly refers to a type of dark, malty beer brewed in a specific style.

(e) is incorrect, since the beer first referred to as the style known as stout was first made by Irish brewers in 1820.

14. (e)

Although the word 'stout' in its original context could originally mean 'brave', 'proud', or 'strong', the term came to be used to describe a dark, malty beer brewed in a specific style, usually with a high alcohol content, making it stronger than other beers. The beer was initially thought to have healthful qualities, but the passage does not describe the physiognomy of its drinkers. Therefore **(e)** is correct.

(a) is incorrect, as although it is sometimes difficult to distinguish between the two, stout is darker and richer than porter beer, as the passage describes in the second paragraph.

(b) is incorrect, as it is either roasted malt or barley that gives stout its distinctive colour and flavour.

(c) is incorrect, as stout is typically classed as belonging to one of two categories, either sweet or bitter.

(d) is incorrect, as stout is made at breweries thorough Europe and North America, as stated in the last paragraph of the passage.

15. (e)

Strong or 'stout' porter beers were popular in London in the eighteenth century, but the first beer considered a true stout was brewed in Ireland in 1820, as stated in the first paragraph of the passage above. So **(e)** is correct.

(a) is incorrect, as the first true stout was made in Ireland in 1820 by the Guinness Brewery.

(b) is incorrect, since it is indeed the roasted malt that gives stout its characteristic properties, and the passage makes no mention of the role that storage plays in its making.

(c) is incorrect, as serious drinkers of stout view added ingredients to boost the beer's flavour as vulgar gimmicks.

(d) is incorrect, as stout is classified as falling into one of two categories, either sweet or dry, as stated in the second paragraph of the above passage.

USING THE DIAGNOSTIC TEST TO FIND YOUR STRENGTHS AND WEAKNESSES

The next step is to examine your performance. Look for patterns. Do you consistently get a certain question type correct? Are you always able to identify the main point of a passage? Do you tend to get detail questions wrong?

The answer explanations will help you here. The explanations describe the reasoning behind the answer choices. Read the explanations for the questions you missed. See if there is a common thread. Be sure to look for patterns among the questions you got right, too. It is just as important to know your strengths as your weaknesses.

Try to evaluate your performance right after you have taken the test. This way your reasoning for picking a certain answer will be fresh in your mind, and you will be better able to identify patterns in your thinking.

What Weaknesses?

Now that you have discovered what you do well and what you tend to miss, it is time to turn those weaknesses into lesser strengths. Use what you have learned to hone your study plan. If you know you tend to miss detail questions, plan to spend more time practicing this question type. Use the strategies described in the next chapters to address your particular weaknesses and watch them disappear.

| PART THREE |

Strategies and Practice

Chapter 3: **Multiple-Choice Section**

- **Six Basic Principles of Critical Reading**
- **Practice Set 1**
- **Multiple-Choice Question Types**
- **Practice Set 2**
- **Kaplan's 5-Step Method for the Multiple-Choice Section**
- **Applying the Method**
- **Postphrasing**

Your performance on the multiple-choice section of the LNAT determines your score. The 30 questions in this section test several skills that are important to a law student.

The LNAT tests your ability to read a passage critically and to grasp both the specific details and the broad concepts presented. The questions also test your reasoning skills. The test makers want to determine whether you understand not only *what* is being said, but *how* the argument is constructed. What assumptions are being made? How well is the conclusion explained or supported?

This chapter will teach you six basic principles of answering questions based on reading passages. It will explain the question types and provide strategies for tackling them. Finally, you will learn Kaplan's 5-Step Method for mastering the multiple-choice section of the LNAT.

The first two sections of this chapter include practice sets and detailed answer explanations. Use these questions to practise implementing the methods and strategies discussed in the chapter. We recommend that you read a section and complete its practice questions in one study session. The third section of the chapter incorporates a practice passage and question set. When you have completed the chapter, you will probably want to review it (or at least those sections in which you find you have weaknesses) several times before your test date.

SIX BASIC PRINCIPLES OF CRITICAL READING

Improving your critical reading skills takes patience. You may not see a dramatic improvement after reading one section. But with steady practice when reading newspaper and journal articles, conscientiously applying the principles you learn in this chapter, you will steadily increase your skill, speed and confidence.

1. Read Critically

What does it mean exactly to read *critically*? Essentially, it means stepping back from the passage and evaluating it as you read, rather than simply taking in the words and accepting them at face value. You must see reading as an active enterprise and confront a passage with your mind fully engaged.

Often when we encounter difficult or wordy passages in something we are reading we tend to glaze over and tune out until we get to something that is more readily comprehensible. When you are reading critically you will become *more* engaged and focused when you come across a particularly dense passage. You will constantly ask yourself questions such as "Why did the author include this sentence? How is this conclusion supported?"—questions that will force you to work through the difficult portions to draw out the meaning.

Here are some concrete ways to improve your critical reading skills:

- *Paraphrase key ideas*: Put the author's main concepts into your own words. These paraphrased concepts are things you might note (in your economical shorthand) on your whiteboard as you read a passage on the LNAT. This is perhaps the best way to improve your comprehension of a passage. Rephrasing the main concepts forces you to carefully analyze what the author is saying.
- *Connect abstract ideas to your own experience:* Particularly in dense philosophical or theoretical passages it can be helpful to imagine a real world example of the idea being discussed.
- *Anticipate where the argument is going:* Stop and ask yourself "What could or must follow?" This will help you understand the author's reasoning. If the passage goes in a direction that you did not anticipate, you may have uncovered a logical flaw in the author's argument. Has the author jumped to a conclusion not supported by—or even relevant to—the evidence? Or you may reveal your own misunderstanding of the passage up to that point, in which case a closer read is in order.
- *Don't be put off by complex words or sentences:* Remember you are not expected to be an expert on any of the subjects that appear on the LNAT. The questions do not test your knowledge on the topic, only your comprehension of what the author has to say. Return to the first strategy discussed. Put complex sentences into your own words to improve your comprehension.
- *Be alert for repetitions:* Not every sentence is a new idea. When authors repeat themselves, it is often because they want to ensure that their readers have grasped an important point.

- *Note keywords:* Reading passages selected for the LNAT are full of structural signals that indicate the logical flow of the author's argument. These keywords allow you to infer a great deal about the content of the passage, even when the subject matter is obscure or the language dense. Keywords fall into several categories:
- *Contrast* signals such as *but, however, although, by contrast or on the other hand* indicate an opposition or shift in ideas. When you encounter a contrast signal stop and ask yourself what exactly is in opposition or in what way has the author's argument shifted.
- *Evidence* signals such as *because* or *since* indicate support for the author's argument. Here critical reading is important. Ask yourself if the evidence offered is relevant and sufficient. Can the evidence be interpreted another way?
- *Conclusion* signals such as *therefore, consequently or thus* indicate a conclusion drawn from the preceding information. The author's conclusion, and *how* it is supported, is of obvious importance.

These signals point to particularly significant parts of the passage, so it is advantageous to pay extra close attention to the surrounding text as you read.

2. Read for Topic, Scope, Purpose and Main Idea

The first third of any passage *usually* introduces the topic, scope, purpose and main idea, as well as the author's attitude to the subject. These are all crucial elements of a reading passage that are almost always addressed in one or more of the questions.

- *Find topic and scope:* Topic and scope are both objective aspects of the passage—that is, they are not determined by the author's attitude toward the subject. If the subject of the passage is the nesting habits of ducks in China and the scope is the impact of development on nesting ducks in China, neither reveals if the author thinks ducks are fascinating, ecologically significant or a public menace.
- As the example indicates, topic is the broad subject of the passage and scope is determined by the limits the author places on his or her discussion of that particular topic. Identifying the scope of the passage is especially important because many answer choices will be wrong because they describe the passage either too broadly or too narrowly. Being aware of the scope can often help eliminate wrong answer choices.
- *Think about the author's purpose:* The distinction between topic and scope ties into the author's purpose. The author has made particular choices about what aspects of the topic to include and exclude. These choices have to do with why the author wrote the passage in the first place. For instance, in our example about ducks' nesting habits in China, the scope of the argument—the impact of development—leads fairly quickly to the author's purpose in writing the passage. The author is interested in discussing how development has affected the nesting habits of ducks in China. From here, you get to the author's main idea.

- *Get the main idea:* Almost every passage boils down to one main idea. The primary purpose and main idea are intertwined. Take, for example, those ducks in China. The author's purpose is to discuss how development has affected the nesting habits of ducks in China. The main idea is simply a more detailed restatement of what the author is asserting.

Development in China has affected the nesting habits of ducks.

The main idea might make a stronger assertion if the passage in question is a persuasive or opinion piece. For example,

Irresponsible development has disrupted the nesting habits of ducks in China.

Most often an author will present the main idea early in the passage, but sometimes it will be built to gradually, after presenting the evidence that supports the main idea. In this case, you may not come to the author's main idea until the end of the passage.

Identifying the author's main idea is crucial to comprehending the passage. When you understand what the author is trying to explain or argue, you can see how the evidence does or does not serve that purpose. Identifying the main idea and, once you have found it, considering how the rest of the passage supports that idea should be in the forefront of your mind as you read.

Not only does finding the main idea engage your mind as you read the passage but identifying the main idea is a very common LNAT question. You will save yourself valuable time if you already have the answer.

To recap, how do you find the main idea? First, take note of the topic and consider the scope of the author's argument. This will lead you to the author's purpose. The main idea is a restatement of the author's main assertion.

As you read, note the topic, scope, purpose and main idea on your whiteboard. These elements will be your starting point for answering the questions for that passage.

3. Get the Gist of Each Paragraph

The paragraph is the main structural unit of any passage. Some LNAT passages will only be a single paragraph, but for those that are more than one paragraph finding the gist, or purpose, of each paragraph will help you create a mental map of the passage. You will become aware of how each paragraph relates to the passage as a whole. How do you do this? Ask yourself:

Why did the author include this paragraph?

What does the transition sentence at the end of the previous paragraph or beginning of the new paragraph tell me about the shift in thought in the new paragraph? Paragraph breaks serve a purpose. A new paragraph signals a new development in the author's argument. The transition sentence often includes keywords that will tell you if the author is developing the same idea, such as *in addition* or *moreover,* or if he or she is introducing contrasting evidence, such as *whereas* or *although*.

How does this paragraph relate to the main idea? Does the new paragraph support the main idea? Does it offer evidence? Does it explain another aspect of the main idea?

Create a map of the passage on your whiteboard: After you read each paragraph make a note that summarizes the author's purpose. The map will help you when you tackle the questions; it will show you how the author develops the main idea; it will also remind you where to look for specific information in the paragraph.

4. Notice Structure and Tone

Two important aspects of understanding the author's purpose and main idea are the structure and tone of the passage. Although topic and scope are objective, the author's purpose and main idea are often subjective. The author has a particular point of view and this is indicated by *how* the author expresses his or her main idea.

The structure of the passage is how the author builds the argument. Some examples of how arguments are structured include:

- passages that contrast differing opinions
- passages that explain a serious problem or situation
- passages that offer a strong opinion
- passages that discuss a particular theory

When you are actively reading you should be aware of the structure of the passage; your map will help you identify the structure.

The tone of a passage is the author's position within the structure. So, in a passage that discusses a particular theory, the author's tone might be persuasive; is he or she trying to convince his or her audience of the validity of the theory, perhaps his or her own? Or the author might have a neutral tone. Does the passage simply describe someone else's theory?

Answer choices for primary purpose questions frequently offer subtle distinctions in tone, for example, for a persuasive passage, you could eliminate answer choices with words such as *explain, discuss or describe* and look for an answer choice with words such as *convince* or *argue for*.

TEST STRATEGY: DON'T OBSESS OVER DETAILS

For school, you are probably used to reading in order to gather and retain information. Reading passages for the LNAT is a different process. You can forget what you read as soon as you have answered the questions about that passage, and you can go back and look for information at any point in order to answer those questions. You should focus your effort on understanding the purpose, main idea, structure and tone.

5. Do the Questions in the Best Order for You

As noted in chapter 2, you can move back and forth between questions within the multiple-choice section. After you have read a passage, quickly page through the related questions. It is often helpful to answer global questions first, especially main idea or primary purpose questions. Doing these first can help solidify your grasp on these important concepts. Other global questions that ask you to identify the tone or structure of the passage are also good candidates to answer first.

Next, you might try any questions that ask you about a specific detail in the passage. Many test takers benefit from leaving the more difficult logic or inference questions for last. These are best tackled when you have a firm grasp of both the broad strokes and specific details of the passage.

However, remember to answer the questions in the order that makes sense for you. If you tend to miss a specific type of question, or you find that you spend too much time hunting around for the information, it might be best to answer this type of question last, when you are most familiar and comfortable with the passage.

The most important thing is to answer the questions in an order that will solidify your grasp on the passage and boost your confidence to tackle the questions that you find more difficult.

6. Eliminate Wrong Choices If You Have to Guess

One or more of the wrong answers on any critical reading question will fall into patterns that you will learn to recognize. Any wrong answer choice that you can eliminate improves your chances of choosing the correct answer. Common wrong-answer types in multiple-choice questions are:

- *Opposite*: Choices that are the exact opposite of the correct choice
- *Outside Scope:* Choices which go beyond the scope of the passage or the particular argument in question. Be careful though: while an inference or assumption must be within the scope of the passage, answer choices for strengthen or weaken questions

may offer new evidence that contradicts evidence in the passage, as long as such evidence is relevant to the argument.

- *Faulty Use of Detail:* Choices that use language or ideas from the passage, but misapply them conspicuously
- *Extreme:* Choices that use words such *always, never, none, all and every* are most likely wrong unless the language of the passage itself is extreme
- *Half-Right, Half-Wrong*: Choices that join a correct statement with an incorrect one; don't be hasty and choose an answer without reading the entire answer

Another wrong-answer tip-off: If you notice that two answer choices essentially restate the same idea, it's a good chance they are both wrong, as there can only be one right answer. But be careful not to miss nuances; some questions test whether you can see important but subtle distinctions between two answer choices.

STUDY STRATEGY: STOP. THINK. PREDICT.

On multiple-choice tests, many students make the mistake of rushing to the answer choices. They read the options and look for the right answer. The trouble with this 'technique' is that it is easy to lose sight of the question—especially when the question is phrased in the negative or you are being asked to find the exception. It is also easy to fall for distracter answer choices.

Minimize the chance of making costly mistakes with the simple strategy we call STP (Stop. Think. Predict.).

Stop: After you read the question stem *stop*. Do not go straight to the answer choices.

Think: It seems fairly obvious, but you need to think about what the question is asking. Put the question in your own words. Paraphrasing the question will help you focus on what is being asked.

Predict: Before you read the answer choices formulate your own response to the question. Having a prediction of the correct answer will help you eliminate wrong answers and pinpoint what you are looking for in a correct answer. You are not attempting to guess the correct answer word for word; this will be impossible with many LNAT questions. But, you are determining the necessary elements of a correct answer.

STP is a short version of Kaplan's 5-Step Method discussed at the end of the chapter. If you take the time to STP before you select your answer choice you are taking control of the question instead of simply hoping to find the right answer.

PRACTICE SET 1

This practice set includes two passages, each followed by three questions. Do the complete practice set in one sitting, keeping in mind—and consciously applying—the six principles of critical reading that you learned in this section. If you have not *just* finished reading the section, skim it again quickly before you start so the principles are fresh in your mind.

After you have completed the practice set, immediately check your answers and carefully read the answer explanations.

Passage 1: Methuselah Gene

In 1998 a scientist at the California Institute of Technology discovered a gene that could extend the life of fruit flies by 30%. He dubbed it the Methuselah gene after the Biblical prophet who lived to 969. Now a self-taught gerontologist believes our mortality could one day be similarly extended. At a conference at Queens' College, Cambridge, this week, Aubrey de Grey, a 41-year-old Cambridge computer scientist, told a research audience that there was no reason why people should not live to 1,000. It sounds like science fiction, but for all that Dr de Grey has been dismissed as a crank, his papers continue to be published in peer-reviewed journals and scientists continue to flock to his meetings. The editor of the *MIT Technology Review* has gone so far as to offer a $20,000 (£11,000) prize to any gerontologist who could put together a serious argument refuting his claims. So far there have been no takers. According to Dr de Grey, such attacks are to be expected. "Traditionally, mainstream gerontologists have preferred to talk about compressing morbidity, but longevity is becoming impossible to avoid," he says.

Dr de Grey, whose day job includes investigating the fruit fly genome, says it is simply a matter of living long enough to take advantage of biotechnology therapies which promise to reverse the tissue damage that comes with age. He calls his doctrine Strategies for Engineered Negligible Senescence, or SENS for short. He has identified seven deadly aspects of ageing, ranging from frayed DNA molecules to tangled proteins that interfere with neurons, sparking Parkinson's and Alzheimer's, to defects in mitochondria, the intracellular structures that power the cell and are vital to the control of free radicals involved in neuromuscular and other diseases. Some of Dr de Grey's solutions, such as using stem cells to engineer new tissues, organs and nerve cells, are already in the works. But his most inventive contribution has been to propose radical solutions. One of these is a body-wide rubbish removal program that would clean up the junk that tends to accumulate inside cells by implanting in people genes from soil bacteria that have the ability to metabolise waste.

But to get to the stage where such interventions are feasible will require a huge research commitment. That is why, in a bid to convince the world that he is really on to something, Dr de Grey is offering a Methuselah Mouse prize of $160,000 to the first scientist who succeeds in extending the lifespan of an adult mouse from two to five—the equivalent, in human terms, of going from 80 to 150. "At the moment the public and many gerontologists tend to put increased longevity in the same bracket as transponder beams—in other words, science fiction," admits Dr de Grey. "But once we meet the robust mouse test I predict scientists will fall in behind my theories and the public will insist politicians make these therapies available to everyone."

Source: "Maverick who believes we can live forever" by Mark Honigsbaum

1. All of these are assertions of opinion **except**:
   (a) Eventually people will live to be 1,000 years old.
   (b) De Grey's most inventive contribution has been his radical solutions.
   (c) It is reasonable that the scientific community dismisses de Grey as a crank.
   (d) De Grey has identified seven deadly aspects of ageing.
   (e) If a mouse's life span can be extended, people will want de Grey's therapies.

2. The writer's **main** purpose in discussing de Grey's work is:
   (a) to critique the validity of his body-wide rubbish removal programme
   (b) to praise and endorse his research into human longevity
   (c) to discuss the probability of increased human longevity
   (d) to explain biotechnological therapies for improving longevity in humans
   (e) to introduce and promote his doctrine of human longevity

3. The writer introduces the prize offered by the *MIT Technology Review* in order to:
   (a) prove that the scientific community dismisses de Grey as a crank
   (b) indicate that de Grey's theory is not easy to disprove
   (c) suggest that scientists are resistant to gimmicky contests
   (d) demonstrate that de Grey's theory is valid
   (e) explain why de Grey's theory cannot be refuted

Passage 2: Trial by Jury

The right of the accused to a trial by a jury of his peers is a hallmark of our justice system, and its is often considered an important safeguard against arbitrary rulings. But is the jury system really such a good idea? Evolutionary biologist Richard Dawkins is not so sure. Dawkins compares the jury system to the scientific method of experimental design to consider if the verdict reached by a single jury is actually less capricious than that of a single judge.

According to Dawkins the principle of statistical sampling is just as relevant to human juries as it is to scientific experiments. He considers an experiment devised by Niko Tinbergen to test if herring gull chicks have a built-in preference for red spots. Adult herring gulls have a red spot on their yellow bills at which babies peck in order to induce the parent to regurgitate food. Tinbergen was interested to learn if this highly specific feeding mechanism was innate or learned. Using cardboard dummy gull heads with different colour spots, Tinbergen measured the chicks' rate of pecking to determine if they had a preference for red over the other colours presented.

For Dawkins the significance of this experiment is what it reveals about the methods used to reach a valid conclusion. He considers various permutations of the experiment with just two colors, red and blue. If a single chick selects red over blue, there is no way to tell if this was a conscious or arbitrary choice. If, once selected, the chick pecks furiously at the red spot, we can't be certain that it hasn't simply "locked on" to the color first selected at random. Dawkins shows that if twelve chicks independently pick red, you have demonstrated a statistically significant preference for red; the chances of getting the same results randomly are only one in 1,024. But, if you test all twelve chicks as a group, this statistical certainty goes out the window. If a group of twelve chicks picks red, it is possible that one chick, who selected red at random, influenced all the other chicks to do the same. In fact this is a likely possibility, as chicks have a strong tendency to imitate the behavior of others. In sum, data must be gathered independently.

And what do herring chicks have to do with juries? According to Dawkins, everything. Juries, he states, are preferred to a single judge not for their greater wisdom or expertise but simply because they are more numerous. However, Dawkins questions whether twelve heads really are better than one. His standard for accuracy, following from the theory of statistical sampling, is consistency over a broad sample. So, if the same verdict is reached independently by twelve people, chances are good that the verdict is fair and unbiased. But, of course, each juror does not reach his conclusion in isolation but as a group with his fellow jurors. The bias for unanimous verdicts and the tendency for one or two jurors to dominate the discussion undermine the principle of independent data making a jury's verdict no more reliable than a single judge's. In fact, according to Dawkins, we might assume that a jury, by virtue of its limited expertise in legal matters, is less reliable than a judge.

Dawkins suggests that the validity of the jury system could be tested in a "Two Verdicts Concordance Test". If two independent juries reached different conclusions after listening to the same body of evidence, Dawkins asserts that this would cast a reasonable doubt on the entire system of trial by jury. Dawkins imagines that two judges listening to the same case would be more likely to reach the same conclusion than two juries. He concludes that if he were charged with a crime of which he was guilty he would take his chances with the capricious whim of a jury, but if he were innocent he would much rather leave his fate in the hands of a single judge.

Source: "Three herring gull chicks ... the reason juries don't work"

4. What does the writer suggest is the **main** reason Dawkins believes jury verdicts are unreliable?

   (a) Jurors generally lack legal expertise.

   (b) One or two jurors tend to dominate a jury.

   (c) Twelve is not a statistically significant sample.

   (d) Jury members do not independently assess the evidence.

   (e) Juries tend to make capricious judgements.

5. The writer suggests that Dawkins uses the analogy of the herring gull experiment **primarily** to show:

   (a) the tendency for a group to be swayed by one individual

   (b) the importance of collecting independent data

   (c) the validity of the scientific method

   (d) the capriciousness of the jury system

   (e) the arbitrary nature of jury decisions

6. Which of the following is **not** an assumption made by the writer?

   (a) Most jurors are not legal experts.

   (b) Jurors who dominate the discussion cause other jurors to agree with them.

   (c) Legal expertise diminishes the possibility of an arbitrary ruling.

   (d) Increasing the number of jurors in a jury would increase the likelihood of a fair verdict.

   (e) The ruling of a single judge is considered potentially arbitrary.

Answer Explanations

1. (d)

This question asks you to make a distinction between opinion and fact. For this type of question you need to consider what evidence is provided for each claim. And keep in mind that you are being asked to find the choice that is **not** an assertion of opinion. If you forget to Stop-Think-Predict it can be easy to forget that you are looking for the *exception* when you consider the answer choices.

For this type of question, you will need a good understanding of the passage's structure. Two answer choices—both **(b)** and **(c)**—can be eliminated right away because they are phrased as matters of opinion: whether de Grey's radical solutions are his "most inventive contribution" and whether it is "reasonable" that de Grey is dismissed as a crank are not matters that can readily be substantiated with evidence and are opinions expressed by the author.

This leaves **(a)**, **(d)** and **(e)**. Each of these is phrased in objective language, so you will need to return to the passage to see what sort of evidence is offered.

(a) is a rephrasing of the author's summary of de Grey's comments at the conference at Queens' College, Cambridge. The author's actual words "there was no reason why people should not live to 1,000", state de Grey's opinion. The author does not provide any evidence to indicate that this is a fact substantiated by de Grey's research.

(d) refers to the second paragraph, in which the author explains de Grey's theory. The statement that de Grey has identified seven deadly aspects of ageing is not a matter of opinion but a factual summation of de Grey's theory. The author follows this statement with some examples of the "deadly aspects" as identified by de Grey. So **(d)** is not an assertion of opinion and therefore is the correct answer.

(e) refers to de Grey's quote at the end of the passage. You can quickly eliminate this choice when you reread the quote. De Grey says "I predict", therefore this is an assertion of opinion rather than a statement of fact.

2. (e)

This is a broad question that you might choose to tackle first as it asks about the author's main purpose for writing the passage—the sort of broad concept you should have identified as you were reading.

There are two important aspects to consider when you answer a "main purpose" question: tone and scope. The correct answer will reflect both the author's tone and the scope of the passage. What is the author's tone in this passage? Does he take a stand regarding de Grey's work or does he remain objective? Although the author mentions others who object to de Grey's work, he does not take a stance either way. He presents de Grey's work in neutral terms. This means you can eliminate **(a)** and **(b)** right away as both suggest that the author expresses his opinion.

This leaves **(c)**, **(d)** and **(e)**, choices that are right in terms of tone. Now consider the scope of the passage. The topic is de Grey's work in longevity, and the scope is to introduce the theory and discuss the reaction to his work. The author does not get into the details of de Grey's theory or specific criticisms of his work, so **(e)** most aptly expresses the author's main purpose.

(c) is incorrect because the author does not discuss the probability of human longevity. That is, he does not address the likelihood that people will live to be 1,000; he simply states that de Grey believes this is possible. This answer not only attributes de Grey's remark to the author, but it is too narrow in scope.

(d) is incorrect because the author does not explain the biotechnological therapies, but simply introduces them. Also, this is only discussed in the second paragraph, so **(d)** is too narrow to express the author's main purpose.

3. (b)

This question asks you to consider how the author *uses* a particular piece of information. In order to understand the author's purpose in introducing this evidence, you need to see how it fits into the structure of the passage.

The prize is mentioned towards the end of the first paragraph. This paragraph briefly introduces de Grey, his claim regarding human longevity, and the response of the scientific community. The author explains that, although de Grey is often dismissed as a crank, journals continue to publish his work, suggesting that his work is still taken seriously despite having serious detractors. In the next sentence the author explains that the editor of the *MIT Technology Review* has offered a prize to anyone who can "put together a serious argument refuting his claims."

The next sentence reveals the author's reason for including this information: "So far there have been no takers." If no one has attempted to claim the prize money, one might assume that it is not that easy to refute de Grey's claims. This assumption corresponds with the earlier sentence that suggests there is a contradiction between de Grey's reputation and his publishing history. The author is interested in suggesting that de Grey's work cannot simply be dismissed despite its seeming improbability. Choice **(b)** best expresses the author's purpose.

(a) is related to the purpose of the paragraph, to discuss de Grey's reputation in the scientific community, but this answer is actually the *opposite* of the reason the author includes the information about the prize.

(c) is a possible reason why scientists have not responded to the contest, but this reason does not fit the structure of the paragraph or support the author's purpose in this paragraph.

(d) and **(e)** are both stated too strongly. There are several reasons that might explain why no one has responded to the contest; the author is suggesting that this is because the editor's challenge is difficult to meet, but he is not attempting to prove the validity of de Grey's theory. Nor is the author suggesting that de Grey's theory cannot be refuted, just that it has not been conclusively refuted at this point in time.

4. **(d)**

This question asks you to consider a specific aspect of the writer's explanation of Richard Dawkins's theory. It is important to note that you are being asked to determine which is the *main* reason. This means that some of the answer choices might be consistent with information presented in the passage but may still not be the best answer for this question.

A careful analysis of the passage's structure will help you with this type of question. As you read you should ask yourself questions such as, "How does the writer present Dawkins's argument?" "What is the main purpose of each paragraph and how do the paragraphs relate to one another?"

In this question you have been asked why Dawkins thinks a jury's verdict is questionable. We know from the first paragraph that his argument rests on a comparison with experimental design. In the next two paragraphs the writer describes Dawkins's analysis of the herring gull experiment. The last line of the third paragraph is a crucial point: "data must be gathered independently." In the next paragraph the writer shows how Dawkins's analysis of this experiment is relevant to juries. The main purpose of this paragraph is to explain that juries do not represent independent data and are therefore "no more reliable" than a single judge. So, the fact that juries do not represent twelve independent opinions but the collective opinion of twelve people is the main reason, according to Dawkins, that they are not necessarily valid, and **(d)** is the best summary of this reason.

A firm grasp of the passage's topic, scope, purpose and main idea should have led you to this answer right away. The importance of independent data gathering is the main idea of the passage. However, let's take a look at why the other answer choices were not correct.

Although the writer does mention jurors' lack of legal expertise, **(a)**, this is not the main reason a verdict reached by jury is not valid. Twelve random people with no legal expertise who considered the evidence in a case independently would, if they all reached the same conclusion, render a valid judgement in Dawkins's view. While **(b)** is a contributing factor, it is not the main reason, in Dawkins's view, why a jury's verdict is not necessarily valid. Choice **(c)** is incorrect because according to the passage, twelve is a statistically significant sample. And the capricious nature of juries' decisions, **(e)**, is an outcome of the fact that they do not represent independent assessments of the evidence, rather than the main reason, according to the passage, that their verdicts are not valid.

5. **(b)**

This question asks you to consider why Dawkins uses the analogy of the herring gull experiment. Again, this question should be fairly simple to answer if you have a good grasp on the purpose and structure of the paragraphs.

We know from the first sentence in paragraph three that the content of the experiment is not what interests Dawkins but rather what the experiment "reveals about the methods used to reach a valid conclusion". And we know that the main point of the passage is to discuss the method of gathering independent data in relation to the jury system. So, the experiment is discussed in order to explain why it is important to gather independent data, as **(b)** states clearly.

(a) is discussed in relation to the experiment but is not the primary reason this experiment is explained in the passage.

(c) is irrelevant. The scientific method is not the subject of the passage, so it is not logical that this would be the primary reason for discussing this experiment.

(d) and **(e)** are about juries. The experiment is not discussed to reveal something about juries. Rather, what is revealed in the discussion of the experiment—that it is necessary to gather independent evidence to come to a valid conclusion—is applied to the jury system to suggest a flaw in that system. A tip-off that these choices are both wrong is the fact that they are very similar. As there can only be one right answer, two answers that are essentially the same must both be wrong.

6. **(d)**

This is a broad inference question. You are asked to consider which of five possible assumptions the writer does not make. This is a good question to tackle last, as you will need to consider each answer choice in relation to the passage. Also, rather than being asked to confirm specific details from the passage you are being asked to consider the assumptions that underlie the writer's argument.

Again a firm grasp on the passage's structure will help you with this question. Let's take the answer choices one by one:

(a) The last sentence in paragraph five supports this assumption; the phrase "by virtue of its limited expertise in legal matters" reveals that the author assumes that most jurors are not legal experts. This is an assumption because the writer does not offer any evidence to support this statement.

(b) This assumption is also made in paragraph five; if the writer believes that the fact that one or two jurors dominating the discussion undermines the principle of independent data, then the writer must assume that those who dominate the discussion in turn influence their fellow jurors.

(c) This assumption is made in paragraph six. The writer states that "Dawkins imagines that two judges listening to the same case would be more likely to reach the same conclusion that two juries". In the previous paragraph, judges are distinguished from juries by virtue of their legal expertise. Therefore, the passage assumes that legal expertise makes it more likely that the same conclusion will be reached—consistency is the opposite of arbitrariness.

(d) Nowhere in the passage does the writer suggest that increasing the number of jurors would make the result of a jury trial any more reliable. We already know that 12 is a statistically significant sample, and 14 or 40 jurors considering evidence still would not make the data gathered independent. So **(d)** is **not** an assumption made by the writer.

(e) This assumption is made at the outset of the passage. If a jury is considered a safeguard against arbitrary rulings, and a single judge is consistently compared to a jury throughout the passage, the writer must assume that a single judge is considered potentially arbitrary. In fact, over the course of the passage the writer seeks to demonstrate that it is a jury rather than a single judge that is more likely to hand down an arbitrary ruling.

MULTIPLE-CHOICE QUESTION TYPES

Although the passages in the multiple-choice section can be on almost any topic, there are just four main question types. Learning these question types and the strategies for answering them is an essential step in mastering the multiple-choice section.

Global Questions

Global questions ask you to sum up the writer's overall purpose or idea. These questions are not the most frequent form on the LNAT, but there are always some. Here are some sample global question stems:

What is the writer's main argument?

What is the main argument the writer makes against…?

What is the main point in this article?

Global questions are good to tackle first, as you should have already identified the writer's main idea as you read the passage. One of the most important things to keep in mind as you answer this type of question is **scope**. Wrong answer choices will often be outside the scope of the passage; they will define the author's main purpose in terms that are too narrow or too broad. The other thing to keep in mind is **tone**; the tone of the correct choice must match the tone of the passage. A choice that describes the purpose of an opinion piece with a verb such as *describe* or *explain* will often be wrong. A quick scan of the verbs used in the answer choices is a good way to limit the field of possibly correct choices.

Logic Questions

Some logic questions ask you to identify the parts of an argument (what is the conclusion, or opinion, drawn by the writer, and what is its supporting evidence). Others ask why the writer has done something—used a particular quotation, cited a fact, made a certain analogy. These questions ask you to consider how some aspect of the passage fits into the overall structure of the passage and the thread of the writer's argument. This question type is very common on the LNAT. Here are some samples:

> The writer uses the example from his own life in order to:
>
> Which of the following best explains the purpose of the analogy in the second paragraph?
>
> The comparison with a game of chess indicates all of the following about the argument except:
>
> Which of the following is an assertion of opinion rather than a statement of fact?

Unlike global questions, logic questions focus on a specific part of the passage; their focus can be as narrow as a particular use of punctuation—for example quotation marks—or as broad as a lengthy analogy. The map that you created as you read the passage will help you in two ways. First, it will help you locate where in the passage you can find the specific information required to answer the question. Second, your analysis of the passage's structure has helped you understand how the author has crafted the argument.

This understanding is critical for logic questions. You are being asked to consider not the *content* of the passage but the *reasoning* behind the content. If you have determined the purpose behind each paragraph, you will be able to see how one aspect of that paragraph serves the overall purpose. In many cases, the correct choice will in some way reflect the main purpose of the paragraph.

Inference Questions

In addition to logic questions, inference questions are the other most frequent question type on the LNAT. An inference question is another way of testing your understanding of the writer's argument. Again, the focus is on the structure not the content of the passage. An inference, also called an "assumption" in the questions, is a statement that *must be true* based on the passage but one that is not stated explicitly. To answer an inference question you need to read between the lines. Here are some sample inference questions:

> Which of the following is an assumption made by the writer?
>
> Which of the following **best** describes the view on capital punishment implied in the passage?
>
> The writer suggests which of the following about humanitarian aid?

Sometimes the inference will follow directly from the writer's main point, or it might deal with a less central point. A valid inference is something that must be true if the statements in the passage are true.

It is equally important that you base your answer only on what is presented in the passage, not on your knowledge from any other sources. Because an inference question asks you to consider an idea or statement that is not stated directly in the passage it is especially easy to be misled by choices that might seem true, or correspond with your own knowledge of the subject, but that are not necessarily true *based on the passage*. Always stay focused on the passage, even when you are being asked to think "outside" the passage.

Here are some tips for answering inference questions:

> An inference should not stray too far from the gist of the passage.
>
> An inference should correspond with the tone of the passage.
>
> An inference should agree with the writer's point of view.
>
> An inference must stay within the scope and main idea of the passage.
>
> An inference cannot be denied by, or be irrelevant to, the ideas stated in the passage.
>
> An inference will always make more sense than its opposite.

Denial Test

One way to test an answer choice is to apply the denial test. The right answer, if contradicted or denied, will significantly weaken the argument. Let's try the denial test on this sample question:

> Which of the following statements about genetic engineering can be **inferred** from the passage?
>
> (a) It is a controversial area of study.
>
> (b) It is the most exciting new branch of study in biology.
>
> (c) It has attracted more criticism from the general public than the scientific community.
>
> (d) It has made great improvements in medicine.
>
> (e) It has limited medical applicability.

Let's say the correct answer is (a): according to the denial test, if genetic engineering is **not** a controversial area of study, the writer's argument will be significantly weakened, whereas the argument might not be affected if it is not an exciting branch of study as suggested in answer choice (b).

TEST STRATEGY: DON'T RATIONALISE

Don't waste time trying to figure out how an answer choice *could* be right. The right answer will follow directly from statements made in the passage; you will never have to take the extra step of rationalising the right choice. Particularly with inference questions, intelligent students are tempted to figure out a way to make an answer choice fit. Resist this impulse by applying the strategies in this section.

Detail Questions

Detail questions ask about a specific portion of the passage and the answer will be found directly in the text. These are less common than logic and inference questions, but there are always some in the multiple-choice section. Most test takers find these easier than the other types because they are concrete. Here are some sample detail question stems:

According to the writer, the most important benefit of early childhood education is:

All of the following are part of Gardener's theory except?

According to the passage, the main reason actors 'should never recite poetry' is:

Most detail questions will be easy to answer with the help of your map. Take the first example, if you noted that the benefits of early childhood education are discussed in paragraph three, you can look back at that paragraph for the answer. The third example provides a quotation; in this case, you can really zoom in on the relevant portion of the text.

The second example represents a more challenging type. The question will be answered by looking for information stated directly in the text, but, because this is an *except* question, you will need to confirm that four specific details appear in the passage. So, even though you are looking for information provided directly in the text, your search for the correct answer might take you all over the passage.

Even though this question type is fairly straightforward and usually represents an easy point for the test taker who has read the passage following the method outlined in the first part of this chapter, it is not always the best type to do first. Although you will have read carefully and will have a good handle on the broad concepts of the passage, you will not have read the passage in order to commit the information presented to memory. For this reason, you will need to go back to the passage to look for each detail in question. Sometimes, especially with a passage for which you can confidently answer a global or inference question, it can be effective to answer a detail question last, when you have already scanned the passage a few times in the course of answering earlier questions. This way you can find the relevant portion of the passage without wasting time, answer your detail question quickly and move onto the next passage with your confidence high.

PRACTICE SET 2

Passage 1: National Education

It was a caricature of postmodern politics. The Conservative benches cheered at Labour's "radical" education policy while Labour MPs sat in sullen silence. Constitutional independence for every school, downgraded local government control and private schools winning access to state cash was "Tory" radicalism, agreed the commentators and Labour heartland alike.

Last week's education white paper showed once again the Prime Minister wearing Conservative clothes, decided the consensus. Further, he was recklessly burying the comprehensive ideal and reintroducing the social selection of the grammar school system by the back door. The consequence of this latest round of fiddling with educational structures would, the arguments went, be for independent state schools, dominated by newly empowered parents, to screen candidates by social class. This adulation of the God of choice would end up further advancing the interests of the advantaged at the expense of the poor.

Both those left of centre (who fear it) and those on the right (who cheer it) believe that Britain is moving to a two-tier education system. Famous columnists whose own children have not gone near a state school warn of the danger of introducing market contracting, the profit motive, constitutional independence and social selection into the state system. They are apparently oblivious to the fact that these are the organising principles of the schools attended by their children.

Others declare, with equal certainty, that all parents want is a good local school at the bottom of their road. But this ignores the extraordinary preoccupation of parents with the nuances of alleged differences between local schools and their frantic efforts to ensure their offspring go to school A rather than school B, efforts frequently reflected in local house prices.

This is "education", a national preoccupation, where the gulf between what the British do and what the British say they want to do is so wide that it eludes honest debate. What we say we want is a universal education system so good that all parents would accept it for their children. There would be genuine equality of opportunity and solidarity between classes. The benefit claimant's child and investment banker's child would happily co-mingle; only merit would count.

What we do is very different. We work the system to give our children every advantage we can and to keep as far away from the benefit claimant's unruly children as possible. The British system is particularly vulnerable to the consequence of this: systemic unfairness that is close to social apartheid, largely because the character of schools so closely follows their socio-economic intake, which, in turn, is determined by the structure of local home ownership.

Some parents don't even bother to work the state system; they simply go straight for the private alternative. Their privately educated children disproportionately dominate admission to the best universities, to Oxbridge in particular. From there, they disproportionately populate every privileged corner of national life. Their achievements are purchased, transgressing every canon of natural justice.

What should be done? If the 1945 Labour government could not abolish private schools, no subsequent government is likely to succeed. In any case, abolition quite rightly would not withstand the first appeal to the European Court of Human Rights. Making charitable status conditional on more social inclusion is one possible route, but that hardly solves the systemic social bias. Most private schools would simply live with increased fees.

Raising state school standards is often seen as the answer, but that ignores the painful reality: what parents are seeking is a guarantor of not just exam achievement but intangibles like social tone, structured classes, freedom from bad behaviour and knowledge that their children's social peer group is like them.

The only chance of weakening the grip of private schools and local housing markets, and of creating more genuine equality of opportunity for all, is to emulate what makes private schools successful in the state sector. That is the heart of the government's white paper.

Constitutional independence offers state schools the same opportunity as their private peers to build and entrench an educational ethos, and more chance of raising money when, for sometimes inexplicable reasons, it is refused by the state. More parental influence will make teaching staff more accountable for performance, just as they are in private schools.

Source: "At last our schools have been set free" by Will Hutton

©*The Observer*, 30 October, 2005

1. What is the writer's **main** argument?
   (a) The education white paper will reduce opportunities for the poor.
   (b) State schools should emulate private schools.
   (c) The education white paper will increase equal opportunity for all.
   (d) Private education is the central problem in Britain's education system.
   (e) Parents do not really want a universal education system.

2. Which of these is an **assumption** made by the writer?
   (a) Private schools are not interested in furthering social equality.
   (b) The education white paper is in line with conservative ideals.
   (c) A private education guarantees success later in life.
   (d) Abolishing private schools would ensure equal opportunity for all.
   (e) Social tone is just as important as academic achievement to parents.

3. The writer uses the phrase "social apartheid" to **suggest** that:
   (a) Britain's social classes are strictly divided.
   (b) Britain's education system has reinforced class divisions and made social equality impossible.
   (c) Britain's schools maintain social divisions through the structure of local home ownership.
   (d) Social inequality in Britain mirrors racial injustice in South Africa under apartheid.
   (e) Social injustice is just as damaging as racial prejudice.

Passage 2: A Generation Gap

According to an article that appeared in November 5 *Guardian*, over the past year 46 percent more Britons filed for insolvency than in the previous year. The number of insolvency cases has risen to a record high, with Britain's total debt having reached a staggering 1.1 trillion pounds. Following the Department of Trade and Industry's announcement of the insolvency rates, the opposition parties criticised the government's role in allowing Britons to rack up this seemingly insurmountable heap of debt. But can the blame be rested at the feet of the government? Surely, the root causes of this financial crisis go deeper than some bad policy decisions.

Vincent Cable, the Liberal Democrat Treasury Secretary, was quoted in the *Guardian* as attributing the spiraling problem of personal debt to "irresponsible lending and aggressive marketing to individuals". Cable called upon lenders to stop practices that encourage people to take on more debt than they can handle, and urged them to "provide greater levels of debt advice". According to the *Guardian* report, industry experts locate the source of the problem in the combination of easily available credit and "a greater willingness among consumers to take on debt without thinking through the consequences".

Clearly, one can only accumulate debt if one is extended credit, and lenders are more than willing to provide consumers with the means to buy now and pay later. But it is perhaps the willingness to take on debt that is the most significant aspect of this crisis. Why is it that some people choose to amass debt at levels they can never possibly hope to repay? Clearly the ease with which one can buy with credit plays an important role. There is a lack of personal connection with the institution lending money that tends to make people feel as if they are not spending their own money, nor the money of any institution or person with which they have a strong sense of obligation to repay the debt. In the days when people had to enter their local bank and apply for a loan in person, surely the loan felt more "real"—an actual contract entered between two individuals—than the moneyless exchange of plastic for goods that characterizes so many modern transactions.

This lack of personal connection, any sense of obligation to the lender, coupled with the eroded cultural barriers to personal debt must also play a part in the crisis. The ease with which people accumulate debt is particularly noticeable in the young. Pat Boyden of PricewaterhouseCoopers reported in the *Guardian* that nearly a quarter of the insolvency cases were filed by people in their 20s who had amassed debts, on average, of 52,000 pounds. This suggests that there is a changing culture of debt in this country; young Britons have a quite different relationship to credit and debt than people of their parents' generation and most certainly of their grandparents' generation. While it is important to address the role played by both financial institutions and the government in exacerbating the debt burden faced by many, it also seems necessary to consider the deeper cultural causes that have caused some Britons to spend their way into bankruptcy.

4. According to the writer, Vincent Cable suggests which of the following two measures to curb the growing rate of insolvency?
   (a) Encourage the government to prevent bankruptcy and offer more debt advice.
   (b) Stop lenders' irresponsible practices and offer greater debt advice.
   (c) Ask lenders to market less aggressively and offer more debt advice.
   (d) Urge people to borrow more responsibly and take more notice of debt advice.
   (e) Make credit requirements more stringent and encourage people to be more financially responsible.

5. The writer's **main** argument about the insolvency crisis is:
   (a) The lack of personal connection between lenders and borrowers is the root cause of the spiralling personal debt in Britain.
   (b) It is not the financial institutions but the impersonal culture of debt that has caused the crisis.
   (c) Young people are less financially responsible than their parents and grand-parents.
   (d) It is necessary to examine the cultural roots of the current crisis in addition to address the role played by financial institutions and the government.
   (e) It is the willingness to accumulate debt that has resulted in the growing rates of insolvency in Britain.

6. The writer suggests all of the following about the "culture of debt" **except**:
   (a) Young Britons are more likely to incur debt than their parents' generation.
   (b) Personal debt used to be less socially acceptable than it is today.
   (c) People used to borrow from people or institutions to which they had a personal connection.
   (d) Today people amass debt with no intention of repaying it.
   (e) If people took out bank loans rather than paying with credit cards they would feel more responsible for their debts.

Answers and Explanations

1. (c)

This is a global question. As you know from the first section of this chapter, you get to the main idea by identifying the topic, scope and purpose of the passage. The topic is the education white paper: This is clear because the writer opens and closes the passage with a discussion of this white paper. The scope is a discussion of the merits of the policy put forth in the white paper. The writer's purpose is to suggest that despite the fears of critics the white paper represents an opportunity to create more genuine equal opportunity in the education system. The main idea is simply a restatement of the purpose; the education white paper represents an opportunity to create more genuine equal opportunity in the education system. Choice **(c)** is the best match and is the correct answer. Why are the other choices wrong?

(a) is the *opposite* of the writer's main idea. You may have been tripped up because the writer does not introduce the main idea until late in the passage. The first several paragraphs of the passage discuss the views of the white paper's critics. As these opinions appear early in the passage, where you can often find the writer's main idea, you may have mistaken the critics' point of view for the writer's own. Be sure to keep clear in your mind *whose* point of view is being expressed.

(b) is too narrow in scope. Although the writer does suggest that state schools should emulate the aspects of private schools that make them successful, this is not the main idea. The main idea must address the topic, which in this case is the education white paper.

(d) is also too narrow in scope and perhaps overstates the case. The writer might agree that private schools make equal opportunity in education impossible, but this is not the main idea.

(e) is again too narrow. This is only a small part of the writer's argument.

2. (a)

This is a classic inference question. We know that for something to be an inference it must not be stated in the passage, but must be true if statements made in the passage are true. This question is a broad inference question in that it does not address a specific portion of the passage. The best approach with this kind of question is to test each answer choice.

(a) is not directly stated in the passage so it is a possible inference. The writer discusses private schools primarily in paragraphs seven and eight. His main point in these two paragraphs is that private schools provide access to "every privileged corner of national life" and they cannot be abolished or forced to be more socially inclusive. Let's try the *denial test*; if private schools are interested in furthering social equality, the writer's argument is seriously weakened, therefore **(a)** is an assumption made by the writer. On test day, you should stop here and move on to the next question, but let's look at the other choices.

(b) is suggested in the first paragraph, but this assumption is not made by the writer but by "commentators and the Labour heartland". So this answer choice tests your ability to discern the point of view expressed.

(c) is stated too strongly. While the writer suggests in paragraph seven that a private education offers special advantages, he does *not* suggest that it guarantees success. The denial test works for this choice. If a private education does not guarantee success in later life the writer's point about access to opportunity is not seriously weakened. He is suggesting that, by-and-large, privately-educated students tend to rise to positions of privilege, but this does not necessarily mean that the schools guarantee their success. Inference questions will test your ability to discern nuances in the writer's argument.

(d) is also stated too strongly. The writer does seem to suggest that it would be desirable, but impossible, to abolish private schools, but throughout the passage he attributes inequality in the education system to both private schooling and the structure of local home ownership. Therefore, the writer would not agree that abolishing private schools would ensure equal opportunity, as it does nothing to address the socio-economic makeup of the state schools.

(e) *social tone* is discussed in paragraph nine. The writer states that parents are interested in social tone in addition to exam achievement. This is another choice that tests your ability to discern nuances. The problem here is the wording "just as important". The writer does not suggest the degree to which each is important to parents, just that they care about both aspects of their children's education. Remember that the answer to an inference question will follow directly from the passage; resist the temptation to read things into the passage that are not supported by the text.

3. (b)

This is a logic question that asks you to consider why the author has used a particular phrase. First you need to find this phrase; it appears in paragraph six. The main purpose of the paragraph is a good place to start with a logic question; the writer's purpose in using some particular language is often related to the main purpose of the paragraph.

This paragraph describes the roots of the unfairness of the British education system. Why is the system unfair? Because, according to the writer, local home ownership determines the character of schools. Try putting this in your own words; you might say schools in wealthy areas are better than schools in poor areas. You should also consider what a phrase such as "social apartheid" itself suggests; it is a provocative way of describing the division between Britain's social classes. The correct answer will get at both the purpose and the tone of the language. In the sentence in which the phrase "social apartheid" appears, the author describes the divisive effect the school system has on the social classes, in strong terms. Choice **(b)** most aptly expresses the author's purpose and the tone of the language.

(a) fails to consider the author's purpose in using the phrase, which is to say something about the effect of the school system on the social classes.

(c) distorts the writer's point. According to this section of the passage, the character of schools is largely determined by local home ownership. The writer does mention the correlation between good schools and the price of housing in paragraph four, but the schools themselves are not actively affecting the housing market as this choice suggests. Rather it is parents' interest in good schools that drives up house prices. Resist the temptation to rationalise. The answer must come directly from ideas expressed in the passage, not from your own thoughts or analysis of the information presented.

(d) strays too far from the passage. Apartheid is a term associated with South Africa, but the author is not attempting to make a comparison with that regime. He is merely using an evocative term that has entered the lexicon to make a strong point about Britain's school system.

(e) also goes too far. The author is not concerned with making a comparison with racial injustice. The question of race does not enter into the argument presented in the passage. Remember, most answers will not stray too far from the writer's main point.

4. (c)

This is a straightforward detail question. The phrasing of the question might have thrown you; the test maker uses the word "suggests", which sounds like an inference question, but the key phrase is "According to the writer". "Suggests" in this case refers to the government official's proposal. When a question says "according to …" you know you can find the answer directly in the passage.

Vincent Cable is introduced in the second paragraph. The writer states that he holds lenders responsible for the crisis and has "called upon lenders" not to encourage people to take on too much debt and urged them to provide more debt advice. The correct answer must involve lenders. Only **(b)** and **(c)** discuss lenders, so we can eliminate the other options. All you have to do now is choose between "stopping" and "asking". As Cable "urges" lenders to change their practices rather than seeks to enact legislation to make their practices illegal, **(c)** is correct.

5. (d)

This global question asks you to identify the writer's main argument. The key to global questions is to find the answer choice that is right in terms of scope and tone. Your map of the passage will help you.

One strategy is to read each answer choice and check it against your notes, where you should have jotted down the topic, scope, purpose and main idea. Another, more effective, strategy is to formulate what you think the correct answer should be before you look at the choices. This is called prephrasing and we will talk about this more in the next section, but you should have all the information you need to formulate a summary of the writer's main argument without looking at the answer choices.

Look at your map of the passage. The topic is the insolvency crisis and the scope is an examination of the root causes of the crisis. The writer's purpose is to suggest that there are cultural causes that have played a role in the current insolvency crisis. So the main idea is that there are cultural causes have played a role in the current insolvency crisis. In order to get at the author's main argument, you will also need to look at your notes on the purpose of each paragraph so you can see the writer's train of thought.

The first paragraph introduces the crisis; the second paragraph notes that Vincent Cable holds the lenders responsible for the crisis. The third paragraph discusses the willingness to take on debt as a modern phenomenon. The final paragraph suggests that Britons' changing ideas about debt and credit are an important aspect of the crisis that must be considered, in addition to the role played by lenders and the government. Choice **(d)** is the best summary of the argument. Look at the other choices to see why they are not correct.

(a) is too narrow in scope. The impersonal nature of credit card spending is part of the argument. It is also inaccurate to say that it is the root cause; the writer suggests it is one of several causes of the current crisis.

(b) is incorrect because the writer does not suggest that the financial institutions are free from blame. She suggests that there are deeper cultural causes in addition to the role played by lenders.

(c) is too narrow in scope. While the author might agree with this statement, the tone is too strong for the tone of the passage, and this statement is cited as support for one part of the writer's argument and cannot be considered the main argument.

(e) is probably the trickiest choice. It sounds very much like the writer's main idea; however, it is stated too strongly. The writer suggests that the willingness to take on debt is "perhaps" the most significant aspect of the crisis, but the passage does not support the conclusion that it is the only cause of the crisis.

6. (d)

This broad inference question asks you consider five possible assumptions and determine which one the writer does *not* make. You will need to consider each answer choice. The work you did on the last question will help you as you will need to have a firm grasp on the writer's argument in order to determine which assumptions must be true if the writer's argument is true. Let's take them in order.

(a) is in the last paragraph. In order for the writer's argument about the culture of debt to be true this assumption must be true. The writer does not make a direct statement about the likelihood of young people accruing debt as compared to their parents, but her discussion of the ease with which young people build up debt and her statement about young peoples' changing relationship to credit and debt rely on this assumption.

(b) is in the phrase "the eroded cultural barriers to personal debt" in the last paragraph. If personal debt was just as acceptable say forty years ago, the writer's phrase cannot be true. Therefore, following the denial test, in order for the writer's argument to be true the assumption stated in **(b)** must be true.

(c) is at the end of paragraph three. The writer compares the "days when" people had to enter a bank to borrow on credit versus modern transactions in which people exchange plastic for goods. The underlying assumption in this sentence and the first sentence in the last paragraph is that people used to have a personal connection with the people or places from which they borrowed money.

(d) is in paragraph three. The writer asks "Why is it that some people choose to amass debt at levels they can never possibly hope to repay". The problem with the statement in **(d)** is that it is too strong. The writer says "some"; **(d)** suggests that all people amass huge debts. Also, **(d)** discusses people's intention to repay, which is not addressed by the writer. The only says they willingly take on too much debt.

(e) is related to **(c)**. In order for the writer's argument (that the impersonal nature of credit cards makes people feel less responsible for their debts) to be true, the converse must also be true. The writer must also assume that people would feel more responsible for their debts if they had a personal relationship with the lender.

KAPLAN'S 5-STEP METHOD FOR THE MULTIPLE-CHOICE SECTION

Now take all the skills you have learned in the previous two sections of this chapter and put them together into a plan of action that you can apply to any LNAT passage and question set.

1. Read the Passage Critically.

Use the basic principles you learned to read the passage critically. Read to determine the topic, scope, purpose and main idea. Create your map of the passage, making note of the main purpose of each paragraph. Remember to pay attention to tone as well as structure.

2. Read the Question Stem.

Identify the type of question—global, logic, inference or detail—and exactly what it asks. Look for keywords such as *suggests*, *implies*, *except* or *not*. The LNAT will often use boldface to draw your attention to important words in the question stem, but you should also make note of keywords on your own. Look for clues such as proper nouns and names or quotations to help you locate the relevant portion of the passage as needed.

3. Research the Relevant Text.

Using the map you created on your whiteboard, go back to the passage to look at the language. Take the time to locate the information in the passage, rather than rely on your memory of what you have read. This will help you clear and focus your mind and find the specific details and nuances of language that may be necessary to respond correctly. This step may not be as necessary for a global question, but even when you have identified the main idea of the passage in the course of your reading, you may need to go back to the text to consider the tone of the passage, for example.

4. Make a Prediction.

Without spending too much time, formulate some idea of a correct response to the question stem before you read the answer choices—at Kaplan we call this strategy "prephrasing" and it will help prevent you from falling for distracters—choices that sound right because they include language from the passage but that are not relevant to the question stem, for example. Putting things in your own words is an important way to focus your mind on what is being asked and to hone your understanding of what you read.

5. Go to the Choices.

The preparation you have done with the first four steps will help you to zoom in on the right answer, or at least to eliminate answer choices that are clearly wrong to narrow the field.

APPLYING THE METHOD

The best way to understand how Kaplan's 5-Step Method works is to try it on an actual LNAT passage. For the time being we have only included the question stems, since reading the answer choices is the last step in the method. When it comes to the actual test you will be practised at prephrasing the answer before you read the choices, but for now we've removed the temptation.

Evil Genius

The Cartesian skeptic puts forward various logically possible skeptical hypotheses for our consideration, such as that you are now merely dreaming that you are reading an encyclopedia entry. The more radical Evil Genius hypothesis is this: you inhabit a world consisting of just you and a God-like Evil Genius bent on deceiving you. In the Evil Genius world, nothing physical exists, and all of your experiences are directly caused by the Evil Genius. So your experiences, which represent there to be an external world of physical objects (including your body), give rise to systematically mistaken beliefs about your world (such as that you are now sitting at a computer). Some philosophers would deny that the Evil Genius hypothesis is genuinely logically possible. Materialists who hold that the mind is a complex physical system deny that it is possible for there to be an Evil Genius world, since, on their view, your mind could not possibly exist in a matterless world. Accordingly, a modern skeptic will have us consider an updated skeptical hypothesis that is consistent with materialism. Consider the hypothesis that you are a disembodied brain floating in a vat of nutrient fluids. This brain is connected to a supercomputer whose program produces electrical impulses that stimulate the brain in just the way that normal brains are stimulated as a result of perceiving external objects in the normal way. (The movie *The Matrix* depicts embodied brains which are so stimulated, while their bodies float in a vats.) If you are a brain in a vat, then you have experiences that are qualitatively indistinguishable from those of a normal perceiver. If you come to believe, on the basis of your computer-induced experiences, that you are looking at a tree, then you are sadly mistaken.

After having sketched this brain-in-a-vat hypothesis, the skeptic issues a challenge: can you rule out the possibility described in the hypothesis? Do you know that the hypothesis is false? The skeptic now argues as follows. Choose any target proposition P concerning the external world, which you think you know to be true:

1. If you know that P, then you know that you are not a brain in a vat.
2. You do not know that you are not a brain in a vat. So,
3. You do not know that P.

Premise (1) is backed by the principle that knowledge is closed under known entailment:

(CL) For all S,a,b: If S knows that a, and S knows that a entails b, then S knows that b.

Since you know that P entails that you are not a brain in a vat (for example, let P = You are sitting at a computer), by (CL) you know that P only if you know its entailed consequence: you are not a brain in a vat. Premise (2) is backed by the consideration that your experiences do not allow you to discriminate between the hypothesis that you are not a brain in a vat (but rather a normal human) from the hypothesis that you are a brain in a vat. Your experience would be the same regardless of which hypothesis were true. So you do not know that you are not a brain in a vat.

Source: "Brains in a Vat" by Tony Brueckner

1. According to the writer, the modern sceptic's hypothesis is consistent with materialism because:
2. The principle that knowledge is closed under known entailment implies which of the following?
3. Which of the following best summarizes the writer's purpose in this passage?

1. Read the Passage Critically

It is common for at least one LNAT passage to include a chart or some way of presenting information other than straight text. These passages can intimidate some test takers. The important thing to remember is that your approach is the same no matter how the information in the passage is presented.

The writer of this passage leaps right into his subject matter. Because the passage starts rather abruptly you may have needed to read to the end of the first paragraph before you determined that the topic is scepticism. The scope is the modern sceptic's hypothesis of the "brain in a vat" which is discussed in the second half of the passage. The writer's purpose is to introduce and explain this hypothesis.

How can you tell what the writer's purpose is? When determining the purpose of a passage it is important to keep in mind the point of view expressed. In this case, the writer introduces his discussion of the brain in a vat hypothesis with "the skeptic issues a challenge". From this we know that the writer is explaining someone else's theory. Nor does the writer make any claims about the validity of the hypothesis. The writer's tone is neutral. The passage does not contain any verbs, nouns or adjectives that would point to a positive or negative take on the sceptics' hypothesis. From these facts we can determine that the writer is simply explaining the hypothesis.

So what is the main idea? Modern sceptics hypothesize that we cannot know that we are not just a brain in a vat.

How does the writer explain this hypothesis? Look at the structure of the passage:

The writer introduces the topic of scepticism—we should note that in this passage "skepticism" refers to a school of philosophical thought not run-of-the-mill doubting—by explaining the Evil Genius hypothesis, according to which there is no physical world, just an evil genius causing all your experiences. This hypothesis is rejected by the materialists, who claim that our mind is physical, so without matter there can be no mind. If there is no mind, then there is nothing for the evil genius to control.

This brings the writer to the updated version of the sceptic's hypothesis. The sceptics imagine a disembodied brain, the experiences of which are all computer-generated. The problem, according to the sceptics, is that we have no way of knowing if our experiences are real or computer-induced.

The rest of the passage explains the sceptics' challenge. How can we rule out this hypothesis? The structure of this section of the passage can be confusing. First the writer gives the three premises, numbered one to three, that make up the sceptics' challenge. Then the writer explains the thinking behind each premise. You have to stay on your toes to realize that when the writer starts talking about "premise 1" he is referring to first item in the numbered list.

Your task is made more difficult because the writer explains the hypothesis using variables. As with many LNAT passages, it is a good idea to put things in your own words. Substitute a real-world example for the variables to help clarify the logic. Follow the advice of the passage; pick something that you know to be true. For example, you are reading your Kaplan LNAT book. According to the first premise, if you know that you are reading your book—you are reading with your eyes, turning the pages with your hands—then you are not a brain in a vat.

Stick with the first premise. According to the writer it is backed by "the principle that knowledge is closed under known entailment". It is important to keep your focus when you encounter dense, unfamiliar language like this phrase. First, what does it mean to "entail"? It means that one thing is the necessary result of another. This is a keyword, so take the time to make sure you understand its meaning. You might think of another context in which you have heard the word. For example, the job *entails* Internet research and some writing. So, the research and writing are the necessary result of the job.

So if *S* knows **a**, and *S* know that **a** entails **b**, then *S* knows **b**. Put this in your own words. If Sally knows that she is in her house and Sally knows that being in her house means that she is not in her car, then Sally knows that she is not in her car.

Now take a look at premise 2. You do not know that you are *not* a brain in a vat. The writer explains in the last paragraph that this is because your experiences would be the same whether you were a brain in a vat or a complete human being. As a result of premises one and two, you do not know the "thing that you know to be true". The main idea of the hypothesis is that your only evidence that you are not a brain in a vat is your experience and according to the hypothesis your experiences are not reliable.

Now you have untangled the passage, you are ready to move on to the questions.

2. Read the Question Stem

Remember that you should read through the questions and answer them in the order that makes sense for you. On the real test, you should quickly scroll through the screens for the questions related to the passage—there are two, three, or four questions per passage. Here are the question stems again:

1. According to the writer, the modern sceptic's hypothesis is consistent with materialism because:
2. The principle that knowledge is closed under known entailment implies which of the following:
3. Which of the following **best** summarizes the writer's purpose in this passage?

The questions fall into three types: 1 is a detail question; 2 is an inference question; and 3 is a global question. Many test takers find it easiest to answer a global question first, while the entire passage is fresh in their minds. So continue with the 5-Step Method and answer question 3.

3. Which of the following **best** summarizes the writer's purpose in this passage?

3. Research the Relevant Text

For global questions, you already completed your research when you identified the topic, scope, purpose and main idea and completed your map as you read the passage. A quick review of your notes should be sufficient, but you might want to quickly scan the passage if you are unsure of the tone.

4. Make a Prediction

Before you read the answer choices, formulate your own answer to the question. Your work should already be done for this global question, as you should have identified the writer's purpose on your whiteboard.

5. Go to the Choices

(a) To contrast the Evil Genius hypothesis with the "brain in a vat" hypothesis

(b) To argue that the "brain in a vat" hypothesis is impossible to disprove

(c) To introduce and explain the "brain in a vat" hypothesis

(d) To demonstrate why the "brain in a vat hypothesis" must be true

(e) To discuss the merits of scepticism

Choice **(c)** has the right elements—both the tone and the scope are correct. **(a)** suggests that the Evil Genius hypothesis is given equal weight with the "brain in a vat" when, in fact, the writer uses the Evil Genius hypothesis to introduce the "brain in a vat" hypothesis, which is his main topic. Choices **(b)** and **(d)** suggest that the author argues in favour of the theory; there is nothing in the language of the passage to suggest that the writer either agrees or disagrees with the hypothesis. Finally, **(e)** is incorrect because the scope is too broad. The writer's main topic is not scepticism in general but one particular theory of modern sceptics.

Try the other questions using steps two through five of the 5-Step method.

2. Read the Question Stem

You might choose to do the detail question next because you can find the answer directly in the text.

1. According to the writer, the modern sceptic's hypothesis is consistent with materialism because:

Note the keywords: "according to" means that you will find the answer in the text; "materialism" gives you an idea of where to look. Make sure you understand what the question is asking: in this case, you are being asked to see what the writer says about the modern sceptics' hypothesis and materialism.

3. Research the Relevant Text

Materialism is discussed in the first paragraph, a quick review of which will give you an explanation of the materialists' take on the Evil Genius hypothesis. They hold that the mind is a physical system so the mind cannot exist in a matterless universe. So what is different about the "modern" sceptics' hypothesis? The brain is a physical object; it is just disembodied and all its experiences are computer induced.

4. Make a Prediction

From your research you know that the answer must address the idea that the modern sceptics have created a scenario in which the brain is a physical object, which the materialists hold to be true. Complete the sentence provided in the question stem in your own words:

1. According to the writer, the modern sceptic's hypothesis is consistent with materialism because

   ...the brain in a vat physically exists.

5. Go to the Answer Choices

(a) It is genuinely logically possible.

(b) The mind is a complex physical system.

(c) The brain in a vat is a physical object.

(d) The brain in a vat is disembodied.

(e) It is an updated version of the evil genius world.

The work you did in steps two, three and four will lead you directly to correct choice **(c)**.

(a) is a typical distracter, taking words from the passage that sound correct, but do not accurately complete the sentence. This phrase appears *before* the relevant portion of the passage and is a statement about some philosophers' view of the Evil Genius hypothesis.

(b) is very c ose to being right. It addresses the idea that the materialists are concerned with the mind's physical nature, but it fails to connect this idea with the modern sceptics' hypothesis—the brain in a vat.

(d) is an aspect of the modern sceptics' hypothesis but it does not address the materialists' concern.

(e) is true, but it does not explain *why* this updated version is consistent with materialism.

Now look at question 2.

2. Read the Question Stem

2. The principle that knowledge is closed under known entailment implies which of the following:

The second question is an inference question. It is often best to tackle these last, as they require the greatest depth of understanding of the ideas expressed in the passage. Look for keywords in the question stem; "implies" tells you that this is an inference question. The phrase "knowledge closed under known entailment" means that you will need to focus on the explanation of the "brain in a vat" hypothesis that comes toward the end of the passage.

3. Research the Relevant Text

To answer this question you need to consider the implications of the principle "that knowledge is closed under known entailment". Go back to the passage and study the explanation of the principle. The principle states that if you know **a** and knowledge of **a** entails **b** then you also know **b**. Further, if it turns out that you don't know **b**, you don't know **a**. Although this might suggest that **b** entails **a**, this is not necessarily true. For example, if you know that you are sitting at your computer and if you are sitting at your computer you are not a brain in a vat, the converse is not necessarily true. So, if you are not a brain in a vat this does not entail that you are sitting at your computer. You could be anywhere.

4. Make a Prediction

What does this principle imply? An implication that is supported by the passage is that if you don't know **b** then you can't know **a**. This implication is explained in the text; it is stated in premises 2 and 3 of the "brain in a vat" hypothesis. As it is not stated as part of the principle, this is one possible correct answer.

5. Go to the Choices

(a) if **a** entails **b** then **b** must be true.

(b) if **a** entails **b** then **b** must entail **a.**

(c) if **a** entails **b** then **a** must be true.

(d) if **a** entails **b, b** does not necessarily entail **a.**

(e) if **b** entails **a** then **a** must be true.

Here is an interesting case where the answer choices do not include the prediction. However, the work you did to get to the prediction has prepared you to find the correct answer. Your best strategy when you do not find your prediction among the answer choices is to consider each possible answer and eliminate the wrong answers.

Choices **(a)**, **(c)** and **(e)** can all be eliminated because the "entailment" principle does not imply anything about the truth of either half of the equation.

This leaves **(b)** and **(d)**. Choice **(b)** is tempting. The fact that if you do not know **b** then you cannot know a suggests, incorrectly, that **b** entails **a**. However, if you substitute a real situation for the variables you will quickly find that **b** does not necessarily entail **a**. Another way to test the validity of this answer choice is with the denial test. Does the premise still hold true if **b** does *not* entail **a**? Yes. If you are not a brain in a vat (**b**) it is not a necessary result (entailment) that you are sitting at your computer (**a**). So **(d)** is a correct implication of the premise. It is not something you would necessarily be able to predict because it is essentially a negative implication. However, by doing the work of the first steps you have a firm grasp on the text and the possible implications of the premise.

POSTPHRASING

Prephrasing or predicting is an effective strategy for avoiding distracters and zeroing in on the right answer. Now let's talk about postphrasing.

Many students think that all they need to do to prepare for a standardised test is to take sample tests. They think that familiarity with the test format and practice, practice, practice will prepare them adequately for test day.

But familiarity is only part of your preparation. If you make mistakes in your practice exercises and don't take the time to understand where you went wrong, you are missing a crucial aspect of your LNAT preparation.

STUDY STRATEGY: POSTPHRASING

Postphrasing is an important strategy for ensuring you learn from your mistakes.

1. **Go back to one of the practice sets, preferably one you did not do recently, and circle the correct answers for the question set for one passage. Don't read the explanations.**
2. **Go to the answer choices and jot down why each wrong choice is incorrect.**
3. **Compare your explanations with the explanations provided in the book.**

If your rationale for determining that a choice was wrong does not match, you are not thinking like a test-maker yet. Postphrasing can help you cement your understanding of the questions and the principles explained in this chapter. It will take your practice to the next level and make sure you are getting the most out of the detailed answer explanations found in this book.

Congratulations. By completing this chapter you have made great progress toward gaining a high score on the LNAT. We suggest that you review the chapter several times before your test date. When you feel very comfortable with the strategies you have learned in this chapter, take the full-length practice test. Then postphrase the wrong answer choices before you read the explanations, in order to get the most out of the practice test.

Now you are ready to tackle the LNAT essay!

IF YOU LEARNED ONLY TWO THINGS IN THIS CHAPTER ...

1. Follow Kaplan's 5-Step Method for the Multiple-Choice Section:
    - Read the passage critically.
    - Read the question stem.
    - Research the relevant text.
    - Make a prediction.
    - Go to the answer choices.
2. Maximize what you learn from your practice by postphrasing.

Chapter 4: **The Essay**

- **What the Readers Are Not Looking For...**
- **...And What They Are**
- **Essay Topics**
- **Make Your Point Economically**
- **Kaplan's Five Steps to an Excellent Essay**
- **Preparing for the Essay Section**

Unlike the multiple-choice section, which is scored, the essay section of the LNAT will be passed along unmarked to the universities you selected to receive your results when you registered.

This does not mean it is unimportant. Each university uses your LNAT score and your essay in the way that best suits its admission system. A well-written LNAT essay could tip the scales in your favour (or a poor one against you) in a close decision, so it is worth preparing for this portion of the test.

Can you prepare for the writing section? Absolutely, and Kaplan can help.

First, you should learn and internalise what universities are interested in when they review LNAT essays.

Second, you should practise writing essays of the desired length within the time period you will have when you sit for the LNAT.

An understanding of what universities are looking for, familiarity with the types of questions you can expect on the LNAT, and a practiced ability to write to a specific length in a specific time period will all help you put forth your best effort.

WHAT THE READERS ARE NOT LOOKING FOR...

The purpose of the essay section is to test candidates' ability to construct an economical argument and their command of the English language. The essay is not used to test your knowledge of any particular subject but rather your intellectual ability and communications skills. Of course, it will be easier to write an intelligent essay if you have a general understanding of the issues of the day. The reading and argument analysis you have been doing to practise for the multiple-choice questions will help you on the essay portion as well.

The LNAT essay is quite different from essays you are probably used to writing for most of your classes. For the LNAT, you can still write a fine essay even if you had your facts completely wrong. As long as you clearly state your assumptions in your essay, it is entirely possible to write a strong essay based on faulty assumptions. Although this might surprise you, the people who will be reading your essay are interested not in what you know but in your ability to convey a reasoned argument.

Similarly, the universities are not especially interested in passing value judgements on your opinions. They are not reading to find out whether you take the "right" or "wrong" stand on recycling, for example, but how well you are able to defend whatever position you take. So, even if you think recycling is very important, you might write an effective essay arguing that recycling is an inadequate solution to the problems of waste management.

...AND WHAT THEY ARE

If they don't care about what you know or what you think, what exactly are they looking for? The universities are interested in whether you can successfully defend a particular point of view. They will reward an essay in which the writer takes a firm position and makes a strong defence. A writer who does not commit to one position will not build a strong argument.

The universities are also interested in economy of expression. The ideal LNAT essay is 500 to 600 words long. Learn to recognize that length. For example, the beginning of this chapter is already more than 500 words long.

Economy of expression is important because it demonstrates your ability to select and organise relevant ideas; to compose carefully, avoiding digression and repetition; and to use language to the greatest effect. An economical writing style demonstrates disciplined thinking, a useful skill for a prospective law student.

As universities are also interested in your command of the English language, it should go without saying that you must use complete sentences; this means avoiding bulleted lists and most especially any language shortcuts that you might be accustomed to using when typing text messages and the like.

WRITING STRATEGY: THINK OPPORTUNITY

The Essay offers an opportunity to demonstrate such skills as your ability to:

- meet a strict time deadline
- select relevant evidence
- recognize your own underlying assumptions
- effectively refute alternative arguments
- address complex ideas coherently

ESSAY TOPICS

As you learned in chapter 2, you will choose one of five possible essay topics. Here are some sample questions:

> The Internet must submit to some government control to limit criminal activity and other forms of exploitation. Do you agree?
>
> Do landowners have a right to restrict access to public footpaths on their land?
>
> Television has eroded community ties by drawing people away from public spaces into the privacy of their homes. Do you agree?
>
> What is your response to the view that richer nations should forgive the debts of poorer nations as a humanitarian gesture?
>
> How would you respond to the statement that novels can tell us as much about the world as history books?
>
> Advertising to children by manufacturers of soft drinks should be limited. Do you agree?

You can find more sample questions on the official LNAT website. In general, the questions ask you to take a stance on an issue in contemporary society.

You do not need to marshal any facts to write a strong LNAT essay. Take the question about forgiving debt, for example; while a general knowledge of the world debt situation might help you formulate your ideas, you are being asked to consider this issue in broad terms. You do not need to know which countries owe money, the political situations in those countries, or the details of their national economy to discuss the positive or negative outcomes of allowing countries not to pay back money borrowed from wealthier nations.

Some questions ask about quite specific issues, like public access to private land; others address such broad concepts as the ability of novels to tell us about the world. Try planning and writing essays using these sample questions to determine which types of question you handle best. For example, you may find that you are better able to address specific topics rather than the more general issues, or that you prefer current social issues rather than broad historical ones. This knowledge will help you select the best question of the five options during the real test.

MAKE YOUR POINT ECONOMICALLY

The key to a successful LNAT essay is efficiency, and that means organization. You have forty minutes to write between 500 and 600 words. This gives you enough time to plan your essay carefully. Use your whiteboard to plan your essay before you begin typing. There are several important techniques for writing a successful essay that we will review using an actual LNAT essay topic. (You'll find more help with the writing process in Part Five.)

Readers for universities will not be impressed with a random peppering of fancy words, either. This does not mean that you cannot use sophisticated language if it is appropriate, but it does mean that rhetorical flourishes will not make up for poorly organised thoughts. In most cases straightforward language is best suited to the economical style of the LNAT essay.

WRITING STRATEGY: BEING CLEAR

The LNAT essay is not the place to try to convince the world of anything, or to try and write the great 21st century novel. Here are some specific guidelines to improving your writing under timed conditions:

- **Generally use straightforward sentence structures, but use structural variation to emphasize important points. Too many complex sentences may confuse your ideas and spawn errors.**
- **Be assertive: write in the active voice and state your ideas firmly.**
- **Avoid redundancy and wordiness; they only draw attention to how little you have actually said.**
- **Edit out vagueness and ambiguity.**

KAPLAN'S 5-STEPS TO AN EXCELLENT ESSAY

Now, let's use the last question in our list of question samples to demonstrate how to plan and write an effective LNAT essay.

1. Select a topic and decide your position.

Remember, even though the question asks "Do you agree?", you do not have to write an essay expressing your true personal opinion. Many people find that they become disorganised when they write on topics about which they have a strong emotional response. It is possible that you can write a more focused essay from a point of view that opposes your own.

The discussion in this section will be more meaningful to you if you take a few moments to select a topic from among the five offered, and decide what your position would be.

For our example, we'll argue that advertising to children by soft-drink manufacturers should be limited.

2. Make a rough outline.

Begin to formulate your argument with a rough outline. What are the main thoughts you want to express? Again, the following discussion will be more meaningful if you stop and jot down an outline of your own before reading any further.

We've written out some ideas here, but remember to develop your own shorthand, and keep the notations to as little as you need to work from as you write:

> Soft drinks are harmful to children. They have no nutritional value and have been linked to unhealthy weight gain.
>
> Children are particularly vulnerable to advertising. They are less capable than adults of understanding the difference between advertising and "regular" programming.
>
> Manufacturers will not stop advertising to children voluntarily because these advertising campaigns are effective. Therefore, limits should be imposed on their actions.
>
> Manufacturers should not be allowed to advertise during children's television programming, nor should they be allowed to advertise their products using characters from children's programming.

3. Develop detail in your outline.

Develop the ideas you jotted down in your rough outline. Spend some time on this. It will guide your writing and keep your thoughts organized. You should spend between five and ten minutes planning your essay. Don't worry about making it a formal outline in your practice tests or on test day—we've only done so here to make it easier for you to follow. Just collect related ideas together with relevant supporting details.

Using only a few minutes, develop your own outline further here:

Here's our expanded outline:

I. Advertising to children for soft drinks should be limited

   A. Compare limits on cigarette companies

   B. Soft drinks harmful to children

      a. No nutritional value

      b. Link to childhood obesity

      c. Sugar-free potentially cancer causing

   C. Cannot rely on advertisers to protect children, government must intervene.

II. Advertising to children is especially powerful

   A. Children not intellectually capable

   B. Advertisers take advantage of vulnerability

      a. adverts look like the programmes

      b. use characters appealing to children

      c. tie-in their product with children's films

   C. Because children are particularly susceptible, advertisers will not curtail voluntarily

III. Government needs to regulate marketing of soft drinks to children.

   A. Government's role to safeguard public, especially children, from unfair business practice

   B. Public interest to promote health in children

      a. Childhood obesity predicts adult health problems

      b. Health costs are borne by the public

      c. Healthy children less likely to have social problems as adults

   C. Government effective in changing public health problems, such as cigarette smoking, through limits on advertising

IV. Conclusion

   A. Suggestions for change

      a. No advertising of soft drinks during children's programming

      b. No use of children's characters

      c. Public health messages about the dangers

B. Potential benefits of such changes

a. Improvement in children's health

b. Long term reduction in national health costs

C. Summation: Soft drink manufacturers won't voluntarily cease advertising to children, a large market for their product that responds well to advertising. Government therefore has to act in the interest of the public and enact policies that will benefit the next generation and the nation as a whole.

WRITING STRATEGY: CREATE AN EFFECTIVE OUTLINE

Some guidelines will help ensure a complete, organized essay structure:

- Put your opinion statement in your outline so you will not forget to state this clearly, in the first paragraph, when you write your essay.
- State in your outline any assumptions you have made in support of your argument; remember, your assumptions don't necessarily have to be supported.
- Each main idea should have two or three sub-items in support of it; this indicates that the idea is fully developed.
- Make sure each paragraph follows on from the previous one; sketch out transition sentences in your outline to make sure your logic is clear.
- Close your outline with a concluding statement that is supported by the points included in your outline. Even if you are introducing a new thought, which can sometimes make an effective conclusion, it should follow directly from the ideas presented.
- When you have completed your outline, review it to make sure your essay does not stray from the topic. Each paragraph should build from your statement of opinion and lead to your conclusion–both of which must address the question.

4. Write a Rough Draft.

When you write your essay follow your outline closely. Avoid the temptation to change your point of view or insert new but undeveloped arguments. In a timed essay, those are two formulas for disorganization and internal contradictions.

With a carefully planned outline, you can focus on the clarity and compactness of your language as you write. This is not to say that you won't discover some nuance of your argument as you write that will cause you to add an idea that you did not include in your outline. Your outline is not set in stone, but it should serve as your guidepost as you write.

Read each paragraph after you have completed it. Make sure it follows your outline, and that you have avoided both redundancy and digression. However, don't worry about getting the language perfect in your rough draft. The purpose of the rough draft is to put your outline into full sentences, which you will refine when you edit.

The LNAT computer includes a word count (as does the word processing system you use in your practice). Keep an eye on it as you write. (If you practise writing essays out by hand, learn how many words in your handwriting fill a standard lined page.) If your outline has four main ideas, each main idea should be covered in about 125 to 150 words. If you find that you have already written 200 words and you are still on your first main idea, then you should go back and look for places to cut. If you are more or less on target, don't worry about the exact length until you are finished.

If you started with a solid outline, you should only need about twenty minutes to write your draft, leaving you enough time to edit carefully. Keep an eye on the time remaining as you work.

Again, to make the discussion more meaningful, write your own essay, based on the outline you developed, either in the following space or on your computer (using only basic word processing, as you will on the exam).

Here is a rough draft based on the outline we created above:

> The manufacturers of soft drinks should be limited from advertising to children. Soft drinks have been proven to be harmful to children, and the public cannot rely on companies to cut back on their marketing efforts voluntarily. Years ago it may have seemed implausible that the manufacturers of cigarettes could be made to print warnings on their packaging that the product for sale was in fact a deadly killer. Yet, these warning labels are now ubiquitous and accepted as the price a manufacturer has to pay for continuing to produce a harmful product. While soft drinks may not seem to be as lethal as cigarettes, they can do significant damage to the health of a child.
>
> First, it is quite clear that soft drinks have no nutritional value. However, they are not simply lacking in any positive health benefits. The sugar-laden drinks add a large number of useless calories to the diet and they have been shown to be a contributing factor to childhood obesity. Drinking sugar-free fizzy drinks is not an acceptable solution. These drinks replace sugar with known or potential carcinogens, and still do not add any nutritional value to children's diets. Because the soft drink industry makes a profit from marketing these harmful drinks to children, they will not stop pushing their product voluntarily.
>
> Children are an especially easy target for advertisers. They are not intellectually developed enough to recognize or critique advertisements. When adverts for soft drinks air during children's programming, and when the adverts are designed in the same style as the regular programmes, children view the advertisement with the same interest as the programme. Further, they accept the advertiser's message at face value. Because children are so susceptible to advertising, manufacturers will not curtail this effective marketing strategy voluntarily.
>
> Does this mean that the government should intervene? Given the negative health effects of soft drinks and the vulnerability of children, the government has a responsibility to safeguard the public. It is in the public interested to promote health in children. Childhood obesity has been shown to lead to adult obesity, which itself is associated many health problems including heart disease, high blood pressure, and diabetes. Many of the health costs of these diseases are borne by the public. There are also social effects of obesity, because of the stigma associated with being overweight. Measures that attempt to prevent health and social problems are a necessary role of government. Moreover, the government has proven itself effective at influencing public health by imposing limits and regulations on the manufactures of products that are harmful to the public health.

While reducing the advertising of soft drinks to children may seem like a drop in the ocean when one considers children's access to sweets and other unhealthy foods, it may have a significantly positive effect on children's health. There are three simple measures that the government could enact that would help parents curb their children's appetite for soft drinks. First, the government could ban advertising from soft drinks during children's television programming. Second, it could make it illegal to use characters from children's games, programmes, and films to advertise soft drinks. And finally, the government could make manufacturers place warning labels on its product indicating that drinking soft drinks has known harmful effects on one's health.

The potential benefits of these small changes are twofold. If children are not bombarded with messages that encourage them to drink soft drinks, it is likely that their consumption will decrease. A decrease in soft drink consumption by children will result in improved health. From the government's point of view, aside from the humanitarian interest in the welfare of the nation's children, there will be a reduction in the national health costs in the long term. As these are two important benefits and we cannot expect soft drink manufacturers to voluntarily cease advertising to children, the government must act in the public interest and enact this policy that will benefit the next generation and the nation as a whole.

Word Count: 667

5. Revise and Edit Your Essay.

Your final step is to edit your rough draft. Leave yourself ten minutes for this step—enough time to tighten your language and make sure your argument is logical and well substantiated.

Even with a carefully planned outline, it is easy to stray off topic as you write. The editing stage is your opportunity to rein in your argument where necessary. We have edited the rough draft of our soft drink essay, showing the edits: deletions are marked with strikethrough and insertions are underlined.

Editing one's own work takes a clear head. Read your essay, word-by-word, as if you were grading someone else's work, asking yourself the same kinds of questions that you ask as you critically read a multiple-choice passage: What does this sentence add? Does it proceed naturally from what came before it? Where does it lead? In addition, you should consider whether each sentence is as clear and concise as it could be.

Before you continue, go back and edit your own essay. Then compare your work with ours.

In the essay we've written, you know right away that the language needs to be trimmed to bring it down to between 500 and 600 words. This should not be cause for alarm. It is generally easier to cut than to add words.

> ~~The m~~Manufacturers of soft drinks should be ~~limited~~ prohibited from advertising to children. Soft drinks have been proven to be harmful to children, and the public cannot rely on companies to *voluntarily* cut back on their marketing efforts ~~voluntarily~~. ~~Years ago it may have seemed implausible that the manufacturers of cigarettes could be made to print warnings on their packaging that the product for sale was in fact a deadly killer. Yet, these warning labels are now ubiquitous and accepted as the price a manufacturer has to pay for continuing to produce a harmful product. While soft drinks may not seem to be as lethal as cigarettes, they can do significant damage to the health of a child~~. First, it is quite clear that soft drinks have no nutritional value. However, they are not simply lacking in any positive health benefits. The sugar-laden drinks add ~~a large number of~~ useless calories to the diet and ~~they~~ have been shown to be a contribute~~ing~~ ~~factor~~ to childhood obesity. ~~Drinking~~*Nor are* sugar-free fizzy drinks ~~is not~~ an acceptable ~~solution~~ substitute. These drinks replace sugar with known or ~~potential~~suspected carcinogens~~, and still do not add any nutritional value to children's diets. Because the soft drink industry makes a profit from marketing these harmful drinks to children, they will not stop pushing their product *voluntarily*~~ If we accept that soft drinks are harmful to children, we must agree that marketing campaigns that are directed at enticing children to consume these noxious beverages should be prevented.
>
> This is especially true because children ~~*Children*~~ are ~~an especially easy target for advertisers~~ so vulnerable to advertising. They are not intellectually developed enough to recognize or critique advertisements. ~~When adverts for soft drinks air during children's programming, and when the adverts are designed in the same style as the programmes, children view the advertisement with the same interest as the programme. Further, they~~, and generally accept the advertiser's message at face value. Manufacturers take advantage of this vulnerability by advertising during children's television programmes with adverts that are similar in style to the programmes themselves and use characters that are appealing to children to market their products. This very vulnerability to advertising means that soft drink manufacturers will not stop marketing to children voluntarily; it is simply too effective. ~~*Because children are so susceptible to advertising, manufacturers will not curtail this effective marketing strategy voluntarily.*~~

Does this mean that the government should intervene? Given the negative health effects of soft drinks and the vulnerability of children, the government has a responsibility to safeguard the public from unfair business practices. It is in the public interest to promote health in children. Childhood obesity, to which soft drinks are known to contribute, has been shown to lead to adult obesity, which itself is associated with many health problems including heart disease, high blood pressure and diabetes. The public will bear the health costs of these diseases ~~are borne by the public. There are also social effects of obesity, because of the stigma associated with being overweight. Measures that attempt to prevent health and social problems are a necessary role of government. Moreover, the government has proven itself effective at influencing public health by imposing limits and regulations on the manufacturers of products that are harmful to the public health~~. While reducing the advertising of ~~from~~ soft drinks to children may seem like a drop in the ocean when one considers children's access to sweets and other unhealthy foods, it may have a significantly positive effect on children's health.

There are three simple measures that the government could enact that would help parents curb their children's appetite for soft drinks. First, the government could ban advertising ~~from~~ for soft drinks during children's television programming. Second, it could make it illegal to use characters from children's games, programmes, and films to advertise soft drinks. And finally, the government could make manufacturers place warning labels on ~~its~~ their products indicating that ~~drinking~~ soft drinks ~~has known harmful effects on~~ can be harmful to one's health.

The potential benefits of these small changes are twofold. If children are not bombarded with messages that encourage them to drink soft drinks, it is likely that their consumption will decrease~~. A decrease in soft drink consumption by children~~ which in turn will result in improved health. From the government's point of view, aside from the humanitarian interest in the welfare of the nation's children, there will be a reduction in the national health costs in the long term. ~~As these are two important benefits and we cannot expect soft drink manufacturers to voluntarily cease advertising to children, the~~ The government must act in the public interest and enact this policy that will benefit the next generation and the nation as a whole.

Take a look at the major changes to see how the essay was brought down to the ideal length and the argument tightened.

- We strengthened our position. We started by talking about limiting advertising to children, but our argument is really in support of preventing it entirely, so we should say so. State your opinion as firmly as you can based on the support you are providing.

- We cut the analogy with the cigarette industry. While such an analogy might have a place in a longer essay, in a piece of this length it is extraneous and distracts from our main point. This was an easy place to cut. We then combined the first and second paragraphs. Here is an example of when it was necessary to deviate from our outline. If you have too many ideas to develop them all in the time and space allotted, delete some—a few well-developed points are more effective than a laundry list of undeveloped ideas.
- We added a sentence to the end of the second, now first, paragraph that clarifies our assumptions—soft drinks are bad for kids—and restates our position—soft drink advertising should be regulated.
- In the third paragraph, we strengthened the transition from the previous paragraph and did a little reorganization. In the rough draft we got the order of the points a little muddled. The revised version builds more logically to its conclusion. Along the way we tightened the language, and inserted words that had been omitted in the original draft—a common problem with essays written under time pressure.
- The end of the fourth paragraph started to ramble in the rough draft; we cut the mention of the social costs of obesity as it strays too far from the topic—soft drinks and marketing to children. We also cut the defence of the government's role and success in promoting public health for the same reason. Again, in the final essay we ended up deviating from the outline somewhat. You may find that ideas that seemed to fit well in your outline start to stray too far from your main point when you elaborate on them in the writing stage.
- We cut a redundant sentence in the last paragraph. If you have made your point successfully in the course of your essay there may be no need to repeat the point in your conclusion.

Here is the final edited version of the essay:

> Manufacturers of soft drinks should be prohibited from advertising to children. Soft drinks have been proven to be harmful to children, and the public cannot rely on companies to voluntarily cut back on their marketing efforts. First, it is quite clear that soft drinks have no nutritional value. However, they are not simply lacking in any positive health benefits. The sugar-laden drinks add useless calories to the diet and have been shown to contribute to childhood obesity. Nor are sugar-free fizzy drinks an acceptable substitute. These drinks replace sugar with known or suspected carcinogens. If we accept that soft drinks are harmful to children, we must agree that marketing campaigns that are directed at enticing children to consume these noxious beverages should be prevented.
>
> This is especially true because children are so vulnerable to advertising. They are not intellectually developed enough to recognize or critique advertisements

and generally accept the advertiser's message at face value. Manufacturers take advantage of this vulnerability by advertising during children's television programmes with adverts that are similar in style to the programmes themselves and use characters that are appealing to children to market their products. This very vulnerability to advertising means that soft drink manufacturers will not stop marketing to children voluntarily; it is simply too effective.

Does this mean that the government should intervene? Given the negative health effects of soft drinks and the vulnerability of children, the government has a responsibility to safeguard the public from unfair business practices. It is in the public interest to promote health in children. Childhood obesity, to which soft drinks are known to contribute, has been shown to lead to adult obesity, which itself is associated with many health problems including heart disease, high blood pressure and diabetes. The public will bear the health costs of these diseases. While reducing the advertising of soft drinks to children may seem like a drop in the ocean when one considers children's access to sweets and other unhealthy foods, it may have a significantly positive effect on children's health.

There are three simple measures that the government could enact that would help parents curb their children's appetite for soft drinks. First, the government could ban advertising for soft drinks during children's television programming. Second, it could make it illegal to use characters from children's games, programmes, and films to advertise soft drinks. And finally, the government could make manufacturers place warning labels on their products indicating that soft drinks can be harmful to one's health.

The potential benefits of these small changes are twofold. If children are not bombarded with messages that encourage them to drink soft drinks, it is likely that their consumption will decrease, which in turn will result in improved health. From the government's point of view, aside from the humanitarian interest in the welfare of the nation's children, there will be a reduction in the national health costs in the long term. The government must act in the public interest and enact this policy that will benefit the next generation and the nation as a whole.

The more you practise before test day, the less likely that you will significantly overwrite and have to make any major cuts to your essay. Ideally, you'll produce a rough draft that is close to the length needed, and spend all your editing time refining the language and improving the clarity of your expression instead. When you write a timed essay, you want to maximize the use you make of every minute.

WRITING STRATEGY: KNOW THE ERRORS YOU TEND TO MAKE

The most frequent problems with student essays are those that result from starting to write without a plan

- lack of a stated position
- drifting off-topic
- disorganization
- lack of development

–and you know how to avoid those.

As you practise learn what types of errors you tend to make, and look for them when you edit. The most frequent in student essays overall are:

- leaving out essential words because you are writing too fast
- confusing shifts in voice, tense or tone
- lack of variety in vocabulary and sentence structure

PREPARING FOR THE ESSAY SECTION

Keep up with your reading. Not only will you be current with contemporary issues, but you can also improve your writing style by studying the example of others. The work you do analyzing passages for their topic, scope, purpose, and main idea will help you understand how to organise and convey your own ideas when you write your essay.

Write practice essays responding to the questions in this book and on the LNAT website. Use these practice essays to determine which question type best suits you. This way you won't waste time during the real test trying to decide which question to answer.

Have someone else read and criticize your practice essays. It is not always easy to see the faults in your own work.

When you write practice essays, mimic the testing situation. Use one piece of scrap paper. Give yourself 40 minutes. Turn off the spell checker on your computer; you may not realize how much you rely on the spell checker until you don't have it.

Make sure you save enough time to edit properly; you should complete the first drafts of each practice essay with about 10 minutes to revise.

Make sure your essay falls within the 500-600 word range.

WRITING STRATEGY: WRITING ON THE COMPUTER

Your essay must be composed on a computer at an authorized testing centre. The software allows for simple text manipulation, such as cut-and-paste. There is no spell checker. Practise writing with these limited tools between now and test day.

If you are not accustomed to composing on a computer, or if your typing is particularly slow or inaccurate, you should make time to practise.

IF YOU LEARNED ONLY ONE THING IN THIS CHAPTER ...

Follow Kaplan's 5-Step Method for the essay

1. Select a topic and decide your position.
2. Make a rough outline.
3. Develop detail in your outline.
4. Write a rough draft.
5. Revise and edit your essay.

Chapter 5: **Getting Ready for Test Day**

- **The Week Before the Test**
- **The Day Before the Test**
- **The Day of the Test**
- **During the Test**
- **After the Test**

Congratulations! If you stuck to the plan you made when you started this book, you are well prepared to sit for your LNAT. What's left to do? You need to get yourself into the best possible shape for the test. There are a few simple things you can do in the week before the test that will make sure you will be able to give your best performance on the test.

THE WEEK BEFORE THE TEST

Even though the practice you have been doing has prepared you for the test, such focused attention on the test may be causing you to feel anxious as the test date approaches. Of course, there is nothing to worry about; after all, you are prepared. But, there are some things you can do to calm any pre-test jitters you may experience.

Rest

Not just the night before but for a full week before the test, make sure you get a decent night's sleep—this means at least eight uninterrupted hours. Ideally you should get in the habit of waking up when you will need to for your test, if you have an early appointment, over the course of the week.

Sleep habits are cumulative. If you usually stay up late but plan to go to sleep early the night before the test you run the risk of not being able to fall asleep and being tired on your test day.

You also need to rest your mind. You should do some light practice—keeping up with your reading or reviewing your practice tests, for example—but you should have completed the bulk of your preparation a week before your test. Cramming during the week before the test can add to your anxiety.

Get Your Ducks in a Row

Make sure you have your confirmation email from Pearson VUE and the proper identification on hand. You will need one of any of the following:

- A current signed passport
- A current signed photocard driving licence (full or provisional)
- A current government-issued identity card that carries your photograph and signature

The name and date of birth on your identity document must exactly match the name and date of birth you provided when you registered for the LNAT. A full week before your appointment recheck your confirmation email and make sure your name on the email matches exactly with your name as it appears on the identification you plan to use.

If you discover they do not match, you can log on to the LNAT site and update your profile. However, you must make any changes before noon on the second working day before the test. So, if your test is scheduled for Monday, then you will need to log on and make any changes before noon on Thursday of the week before. A working day is Monday to Friday, excluding UK bank holidays.

Visit the test centre if you have not already. Make sure you know how to get there so you will arrive on time for your test.

Don't leave anything up to guesswork. For example, make sure you have reliable transportation arranged.

Stay Healthy

Eating well and getting some exercise can help ward off pre-test anxiety. Make an extra effort to eat well—lots of fresh fruits and vegetables and less sweets and fatty foods—during the week before the test. It should be obvious, but keep drinking to a minimum.

Exercise is a great stress reliever. Leave room in your schedule for a brisk walk or some other form of exercise during the week before your test.

THE DAY BEFORE THE TEST

This is not a day to study. Instead relax and, for a change, try ***not*** to think about the test.

Put together everything you'll need for the test:

- Your confirmation email
- Your identification
- A drink and snack to have before the test, if you have a long trip to get to your test centre
- The address of your test centre and any directions you need to get there

If you have to travel to get to your test centre, and you won't be driving yourself, you might want to bring along some material to review on your way to the test. You might make a sheet summarising some of the strategies you learned in this book, for example.

Do something calm and relaxing the evening before the test. Try not to think about the test, and make it an early night.

THE DAY OF THE TEST

Give yourself plenty of time in the morning. Make sure you have a good breakfast.

Read something to warm up your brain. You don't want the first passage on the LNAT to be the first thing you read that morning. The commentary pages of a newspaper might be a good choice.

Dress in layers. You never know what the temperature of the room will be like, and you don't want to be distracted by being too hot or too cold during the test.

Leave for the test centre early enough so that a delay won't make you miss your appointment. If you miss your appointment you will have to register, and pay, again; you will not be allowed to check in past your appointment time.

DURING THE TEST

Here are some last thoughts to keep in mind as you take your test:

- Confidence is key. Accentuate the positive aspects of your performance as you work on the test and don't dwell on any negatives.
- Don't get bogged down on one passage. There are ten passages, and they are not in order of difficulty so be sure you give yourself a chance to answer all the questions.
- Give yourself enough time to make use of the review feature. If you are uncertain about the answer to a question, put in an answer choice but make a note of the question number on your white board and go back to that question when you get to the review screen at the end of the multiple-choice section.
- Keep an eye on the time remaining as you work, but don't be a clock-watcher. You only need to know that you are moving along at a reasonable pace.

TEST DAY STRATEGY: MANAGE STRESS

Don't forget your stress-management techniques during the test. Breathe deeply and stretch as needed. Imagine yourself succeeding.

Believe it or not, you should try and have fun with the test. You are well-prepared and this is your opportunity to distinguish yourself. The test is an opportunity and a challenge, not an obstacle.

AFTER THE TEST

You will receive your score by email. If you take the test on or before 15 January, you will receive an email notification of your LNAT result at the end of January. If you take the test after 15 January, you will receive your LNAT result at the end of June. The universities you selected will receive your score and your essay right away.

Last but not least, now is the time to celebrate a job well done! Even before you have your score in hand you should congratulate yourself for the hard work you did to prepare for the LNAT and for doing your best on the test.

Don't forget to go online and take Kaplan's online survey to let us know how well we prepared you.

| PART FOUR |

Full-Length Practice Test

Practice Test: **National Admissions Test for Law**

SECTION A: MULTIPLE CHOICE

This section is divided into 10 subsections, each having between two and four questions. Answer all 30 questions, selecting only one of the possible answers listed for each question.

Time: 80 minutes

SECTION B: ESSAY

This section has five essay questions. You should select and answer only one.

Time: 40 minutes

SECTION A: MULTIPLE CHOICE

I White Nights and Knights

Besides being one of the world's best-known conductors, Valery Gergiev is a savvy politician. After conducting the Berlioz requiem in the courtyard of the Hermitage's Winter Palace (wearing a baseball cap), Mr Gergiev is as unfazed by questions about the ascendancy of his opera and ballet company, the Mariinsky, over the Bolshoi, its Moscow rival, as by the fireworks that disrupted the performance, almost invisible though they were against the white night.

A big part of the explanation for the Mariinsky's success is Mr Gergiev. The maestro has unlikely origins: an ethnic Ossetian, he grew up in the Caucasus (he gave a series of tribute concerts after the Beslan atrocity last year). He has become Russia's biggest post-Soviet artistic star, his services sought by opera companies and orchestras around the globe.

The Mariinsky and the Hermitage also have each other: "the great museum and the great theatre," as Mr Gergiev puts it. In him and Mikhail Piotrovsky, the Hermitage's director, both have bosses who have hustled through the cultural challenges of post-Soviet Russia. Both men have cultivated foreign partners, and have quickly learnt the dark arts of fund-raising. Mr Gergiev says he picked them up by himself; Mr Piotrovsky says the Guggenheim and New York's Metropolitan Museum lent a hand. The Mariinsky, says Mr Gergiev cautiously, accepts only clean money. Mr Piotrovsky is more phlegmatic: he is wary of the "crooks [who] come to us from all over the world," but ultimately "there is no clean money." Mikhail Khodorkovsky was a Hermitage donor; Vladimir Potanin, another oligarch, is chairman of the board of trustees.

Despite perpetual planning obstacles, the Hermitage and the Mariinsky (known abroad by its Soviet name, the Kirov) are both expanding. The Hermitage, which now has offshoots in London, Amsterdam and Las Vegas, and plans another in Tatarstan, is restoring the east wing of the General Staff building, across the square from the Winter Palace. The Mariinsky is building a new 2,000-seat theatre. Moscow's Bolshoi closed its main auditorium earlier this month for a much-delayed revamp. Against Mr Gergiev's innovations, Bolshoi productions can seem stale, and its audiences sometimes more interested in their mobile phones than in music.

The two institutions' other edge is St Petersburg itself. Mr Piotrovksy gives thanks to Lenin for making Moscow Russia's capital, which helps to explain why much of it is so ugly. Many of Moscow's old buildings have been torn down; others are draped with street-size advertisements. It may also help that Petersburgers run the country. German Gref and Alexei Kudrin, the economy and finance ministers respectively, are old friends, says Mr Gergiev. Valentina Matvienko, the city's governor, is rumoured to be the likely successor to Mikhail Fradkov, Russia's hapless prime minister. And St Petersburg's other gift to the world, Vladimir Putin? "A man of culture," says Mr Piotrovsky diplomatically.

Source: *The Economist*, 14 July 2005

1. The author's purpose in the first paragraph is **most** likely:

   (a) to help the reader understand why Gergiev respects Putin

   (b) to demonstrate why the Hermitage is expanding

   (c) to explain why the Mariinsky is more popular than the Bolshoi

   (d) to show the difficulties of producing an outdoor concert

   (e) to introduce Gergiev

2. All of the following are assertions of opinion **except**:

   (a) Vladimir Putin is a man of culture.

   (b) Bolshoi audiences are more interested in their cell phones than the music.

   (c) The Mariinsky and Hermitage are "the great museum and the great theatre."

   (d) Mr Gergiev is an ethnic Ossetian who grew up in the Caucasus.

   (e) St Petersburg's mayor will probably become the next prime minister.

3. Which of the following, if true, would **weaken** the author's argument in the last paragraph?

   (a) St. Petersburg is an ugly industrial town with a crumbling infrastructure.

   (b) Many Russian politicians are Petersburgers.

   (c) Street-size advertisements posted on buildings detract from a city's beauty.

   (d) Vladimir Putin is not generally considered a man of culture.

   (e) Tourists prefer St. Petersburg over Moscow.

II Extinction of the Predator

Consolidation in the car industry is not as starkly obvious to the consumer as it has been in, say, personal computers. A plethora of badges still remains, as mergers and alliances between firms over the years have simply bundled, rather than destroyed, brands. No fewer than 58 brands survive among the ten largest manufacturers.

The strategy of consolidating behind the brands has not been entirely successful: indeed there is an inverse correlation between the number of brands a firm possesses and profitability. GM may still be the big beast of the industry, but it is no longer in any shape to gobble up others. It has twice the number of brands of its closest competitor, Ford, but is second to last in the profitability league (see the charts).

The two biggest consolidation deals in the industry are also the most recent: the takeover of Chrysler by Daimler-Benz in 1998; and the alliance of Renault and Nissan the following year. DaimlerChrysler has been a flop so far. It has taken years to lick Chrysler into shape, slashing its surplus capacity and reviving the brand with new products good enough to drag it back into profit this year. Meanwhile, top management attention was diverted from growing problems at home as quality slid at Mercedes, which lost its long-standing dominance of the lucrative German market to its arch-rival BMW.

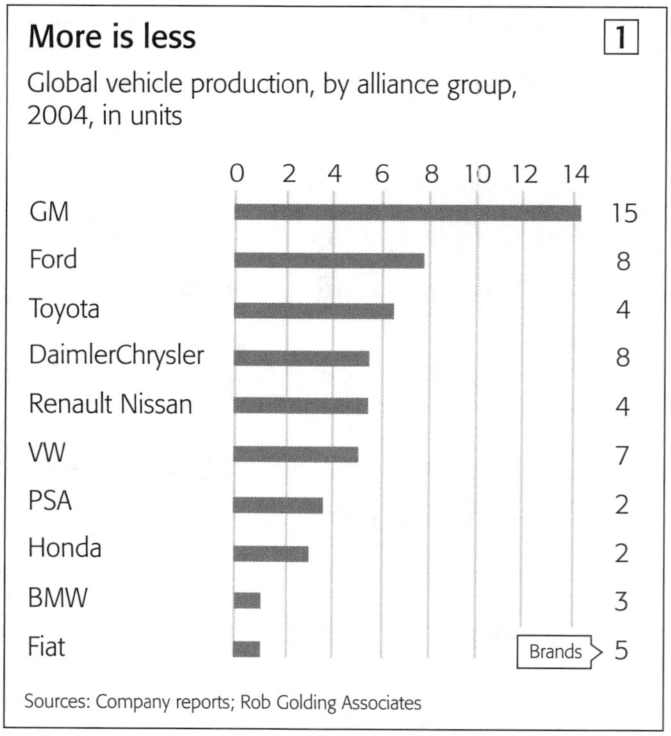

It did not work out that way. Daimler and Chrysler together are worth less in stockmarket terms than Daimler alone was before the merger. This summer the architect of the deal, Jürgen Schrempp, was nudged out of his chief executive's chair (he leaves at the end of this year) by leading shareholders as a result.

Source: *The Economist*, 8 September 2005

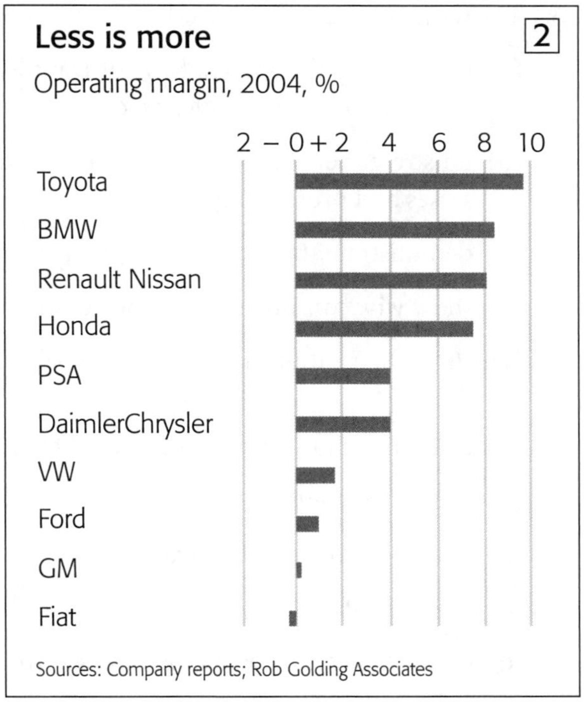

4. All of these are implied or stated in the article **except:**
   - (a) More than four dozen automobile brands are made by the ten largest manufacturers.
   - (b) RenaultNissan has a higher operating margin percentage than Ford.
   - (c) Chrysler's high cost base made it an attractive target for Daimler.
   - (d) The acquisition of Jaguar has not increased Ford's profitability.
   - (e) The alliance between Renault and Nissan occurred in 1999.

5. According to the article, which of the following is likely to be a successful method for increasing profitability?
   - (a) maintaining quality
   - (b) spreading the cost of new technology over a bigger output
   - (c) acquiring companies in the same industry
   - (d) increasing surplus capacity
   - (e) retaining a line of products

6. The writer of the article includes charts in order to:
   (a) explain why the shareholders of DaimlerChrysler removed Jürgen Schrempp from his position as chief executive.
   (b) illustrate the "inverse correlation between the number of brands a firm possesses and profitability."
   (c) demonstrate the need for a high operating margin percentage.
   (d) show why consolidation in the auto industry has produced fewer brands.
   (e) show the relationship between global vehicle production and profitability.

7. Which of the following can be **inferred** from the passage?
   (a) While DaimlerChrysler improved Chrysler, the quality of Mercedes worsened.
   (b) Honda produced more cars than VW in 2004.
   (c) The manufacturer with the most brands is the most profitable.
   (d) GM is looking for ways to increase profitability other than acquiring other car companies.
   (e) The chief executive of DaimlerChrysler lost his job because of the failure of the merger of the two companies.

III Only connect

Landscape cannot, on the whole, be mocked up; cannot be dreamed into descriptive being. Light, water, angles, textures of air, water and stone, the curves and straights of horizon and slope: these are the basic components of natural places, and they combine in ways too subtle and particular to be invented.

This—the dedication it demands—is one of the difficulties of writing about natural places. Another, contrasting difficulty is that landscapes have had too much written about them in the past. For centuries, they have provoked in their viewers an urge to communicate their magnificence. The result is that landscapes have become coated with thick layers of dead language. Wreck-divers use the word "crud," a dialect form of "curd," to describe the submarine minerals which clot around any long-sunken metal object, and which have to be laboriously chipped and leached away before that object can be exposed to sight again. It is—as Williamson knew—effortful work to get back through the verbal crud: to divulge a landscape to what he once called "authentic sunlight."

Increasingly, in the face of these difficulties, British writers have abandoned the effort altogether. Rose Tremain reported recently that she had taken to setting her novels either abroad, or in the past, because there was "no immediate landscape left with which to engage" in contemporary Britain. Martin Amis, who has always paraded his status as connoisseur of urban deprivation—novelist as underbelly-dancer—elegantly rephrased the same sentiment in a 2003 interview. "Our countryside is just bollocks. A friend of mine wrote a poem called 'Bollockshire' about the English countryside. It's all so cute and fake. We have no wilds left."

At the broadest level, the decline of landscape writing must be connected to modernity. So much of 20th-century literature has been taken up with annotating those peculiarly modern sentiments of alienation and its subcategories: estrangement, fragmentation, disconnection and dislocation. It is un-surprising that writing which pays close and respectful attention to place should have come to appear pensionable.

Then there are the three persistent enemies of good writing about landscape. The first of these is cliché. Landscape writing can sometimes seem like the canning factory of style, out of which the same phrases are endlessly issued: the "crashing" waterfall, the "mist-wreathed" forest, the mountains showing "like whale-backs" in the clouds. Try it yourself. Try to describe the last sunset you saw, or the last storm. Clichés—"vivid," "fierce," "lurid," "rich," "wild"—rise eagerly and unbidden to the lips. You quickly end up sounding like Mrs Arundel from Wilde's The Decay of Lying, who insists on "going to the window, and looking at the glorious sky, as she called it."

The second enemy is over-writing. Landscape encourages the pleonastic heresy that more words will always be better than fewer. Too often, writers fall into a Fauntleroyish effusion: the wine-taster's excessively adjectival loquacity.

The third and most serious enemy is a political one. An infatuation with landscape has, at times, come at the cost of a proper sense of human community, or a misprision of human worth. Pantheism shades, repellently, into territorialism. John Muir hymned the connectedness of all things, but disregarded the long Native American association with his adored Yosemite. Williamson's nature-love of the 1910s and 20s later became corrupted into fascism, eugenics, and a worship of Hitler as the "light-bringing phoenix."

Source: *The Guardian*, 26 March 2005

8. Which of the following is the **main idea** of the article?
   (a) Writers should avoid the subject of landscape.
   (b) Writing about landscape has become clichéd.
   (c) Landscape writing has no place in modern literature.
   (d) Writing about landscape is difficult.
   (e) The British landscape is uninspiring to writers.

9. Which of these **cannot** be inferred from the article?
   (a) Rose Tremain would rather set a novel about London in 1840 than in 2005.
   (b) Much writing about landscape is unoriginal.
   (c) The connection between landscape and politics has a long history.
   (d) Landscape has not played the role in modern literature that it did in earlier writing.
   (e) It is difficult to excavate fresh landscape writing from beneath centuries of overuse.

10. In **context**, the term "pleonastic heresy" means:
   (a) lean martyrdom
   (b) terse fallacy
   (c) loquacious misconception
   (d) concise unorthodoxy
   (e) fallacy of redundancy

IV ...and statistics

Theodore Sturgeon, an American science-fiction writer, once observed that 95% of everything is garbage. John Ioannidis, a Greek epidemiologist, would not go that far. His benchmark is 50%. But that figure, he thinks, is a fair estimate of the proportion of scientific papers that eventually turn out to be wrong.

Dr Ioannidis, who works at the University of Ioannina, in northern Greece, makes his claim in PLoS Medicine, an online journal published by the Public Library of Science. His thesis that many scientific papers come to false conclusions is not new. Science is a Darwinian process that proceeds as much by refutation as by publication. But until recently no one has tried to quantify the matter.

Dr Ioannidis began by looking at specific studies, in a paper published in the Journal of the American Medical Association in July. He examined 49 research articles printed in widely read medical journals between 1990 and 2003. Each of these articles had been cited by other scientists in their own papers 1,000 times or more. However, 14 of them—almost a third—were later refuted by other work. Some of the refuted studies looked into whether hormone-replacement therapy was safe for women (it was, then it wasn't), whether vitamin E increased coronary health (it did, then it didn't), and whether stents are more effective than balloon angioplasty for coronary-artery disease (they are, but not nearly as much as was thought).

Having established the reality of his point, he then designed a mathematical model that tried to take into account and quantify sources of error. Again, these are well known in the field.

One is an unsophisticated reliance on "statistical significance." To qualify as statistically significant a result has, by convention, to have odds longer than one in 20 of being the result of chance. But, as Dr Ioannidis points out, adhering to this standard means that simply examining 20 different hypotheses at random is likely to give you one statistically significant result. In fields where thousands of possibilities have to be examined, such as the search for genes that contribute to a particular disease, many seemingly meaningful results are bound to be wrong just by chance.

Other factors that contribute to false results are small sample sizes, studies that show weak effects (such as a drug which works only on a small number of patients) and poorly designed studies that allow the researchers to fish among their data until they find some kind of effect, regardless of what they started out trying to prove. Researcher bias, due either to clinging tenaciously to a pet theory, or to financial interests, can also skew results.

When Dr Ioannidis ran the numbers through his model, he concluded that even a large, well-designed study with little researcher bias has only an 85% chance of being right. An underpowered, poorly performed drug trial with researcher bias has but a 17% chance of producing true conclusions. Overall, more than half of all published research is probably wrong.

It should be noted that Dr Ioannidis's study suffers from its own particular bias. Important as medical science is, it is not the be-all and end-all of research. The physical sciences, with more certain theoretical foundations and well-defined methods and endpoints, probably do better than medicine. Still, he makes a good point—and one that lay readers of scientific results, including those reported in this newspaper, would do well to bear in mind. Which leaves just one question: is there a less than even chance that Dr Iaonnidis's paper itself is wrong?

Source: *The Economist*, 1 September 2005

11. Which of the following is an **assertion of opinion** rather than a statement of fact?

    (a) Dr Ioannidis's study is biased and therefore it could be wrong.

    (b) To qualify as statistically significant a result has to have odds longer than one in 20 of being the result of chance.

    (c) Dr Ioannidis examined 49 research articles printed in widely read medical journals between 1990 and 2003.

    (d) Dr Ioannidis concluded that even a large, well-designed study with little researcher bias has only an 85% chance of being right.

    (e) Dr Ioannidis works at the University of Ioannina, in northern Greece.

12. With which of the following would Dr. Ioannidis be most likely to **agree**?

    (a) If a study arrives at a meaningful result, chances are it is correct.

    (b) The bias of a scientific research should be minimised or eliminated to increase the chances of arriving at a correct result.

    (c) The conclusions of most scientific studies can be trusted.

    (d) Balloon angioplasty is the most effective treatment for coronary-artery disease.

    (e) If a researcher examines 20 different hypotheses at random, he or she is likely to get one statistically significant result.

13. According to the article, which of the following is **not** a factor that contributes to false results in a scientific study?

    (a) small sample size

    (b) researcher bias

    (c) reliance on statistical significance

    (d) not enough time spent

    (e) poor design

V Diarists

Among the vast number of men who have thought fit to write down the history of their own lives, three or four have achieved masterpieces which stand out preeminently: Saint Augustine in his "Confessions," Samuel Pepys in his "Diary," Rousseau in his "Confessions." It is among these extraordinary documents, and unsurpassed by any of them, that the autobiography of Benvenuto Cellini takes its place.

The "Life" of himself which Cellini wrote was due to other motives than those which produced its chief competitors for first place in its class. St. Augustine's aim was religious and didactic, Pepys noted down in his diary the daily events of his life for his sole satisfaction and with no intention that any one should read the cipher in which they were recorded. But Cellini wrote that the world might know, after he was dead, what a fellow he had been; what great things he had attempted, and against what odds he had carried them through.

The period covered by the autobiography is from Cellini's birth in 1500 to 1562; the scene is mainly in Italy and France. Of the great events of the time, the time of the Reformation and the Counter-Reformation, of the strife of Pope and Emperor and King, we get only glimpses.

Much more complete is the view he gives of the artistic life of the time. It was the age of Michelangelo, and in the throng of great artists which then filled the Italian cities, Cellini was no inconsiderable figure. Michelangelo himself he knew and adored. Nowhere can we gain a better idea than in this book of the passionate enthusiasm for the creation of beauty which has bestowed upon the Italy of the Renaissance its greatest glory.

Very vivid, too, is the impression we receive of the social life of the sixteenth century; of its violence and licentiousness, of its zeal for fine craftsmanship, of its abounding vitality, its versatility and its idealism. For Cellini himself is an epitome of that century. This man who tells here the story of his life was a murderer and a braggart, insolent, sensual, inordinately proud and passionate; but he was also a worker in gold and silver, rejoicing in delicate chasing and subtle modelling of precious surfaces; a sculptor and a musician; and, as all who read his book must testify, a great master of narrative. Keen as was Benvenuto's interest in himself, and much as he loved to dwell on the splendor of his exploits and achievements, he had little idea that centuries after his death he would live again, less by his "Perseus" and his goldsmith's work than by the book which he dictated casually to a lad of fourteen, while he went about his work.

Source: Introductory note to the *Autobiography of Benvenuto Cellini*, translated by John Addington Symonds (New York: PF Collier & Son Company, 1909-1914)

14. Which of the following **cannot** be inferred from the passage:

    (a) The author believes Cellini's Autobiography is superior to those of Pepys, Saint Augustine, and Rousseau.

    (b) Cellini's readers learn more about Italian Renaissance artists than about politicians of the period.

    (c) Cellini was not known for his modesty.

    (d) The author believes most autobiographies to be ordinary or even inferior.

    (e) Cellini's aim in penning his autobiography was to memorialise his own greatness.

15. What is probably meant by the author's reference to Cellini's "Perseus"?

    (a) Cellini was a student of Greek mythology.

    (b) Cellini was a citizen of Rome, but his family was from Greece.

    (c) Cellini had a pet named after the infamous slayer of Medusa.

    (d) Cellini likened himself to a mythological hero.

    (e) Cellini was the model for Michelangelo's statue of Perseus.

16. Which of the following is **not** stated in the passage?

    (a) Rousseau's "Confessions" is a masterpiece of autobiography.

    (b) Italy and France are the setting for most of Cellini's autobiography.

    (c) Michelangelo knew Cellini.

    (d) It was not Pepys intention to publish his "Diary."

    (e) Cellini committed crimes for which he was never punished.

17. The author's **main** purpose in the passage is most likely:

    (a) to explain how he translated Cellini's work.

    (b) to give background information about the Italy of Cellini's time.

    (c) to explain why Cellini's work is important and should be read.

    (d) to excuse some of Cellini's more derelict behaviour.

    (e) to demonstrate why autobiography is one of the highest forms of literature.

VI Things Change

There are certain half-dreaming moods of mind, in which we naturally steal away from noise and glare, and seek some quiet haunt, where we may indulge our reveries and build our air castles undisturbed. In such a mood I was loitering about the old gray cloisters of Westminster Abbey, enjoying that luxury of wandering thought which one is apt to dignify with the name of reflection; when suddenly an interruption of madcap boys from Westminster School, playing at football, broke in upon the monastic stillness of the place, making the vaulted passages and mouldering tombs echo with their merriment. I sought to take refuge from their noise by penetrating still deeper into the solitudes of the pile, and applied to one of the vergers for admission to the library.

I found myself in a lofty antique hall, the roof supported by massive joists of old English oak. Around the hall and in a small gallery were the books, arranged in carved oaken cases. They consisted principally of old polemical writers, and were much more worn by time than use. In the center of the library was a solitary table with two or three books on it, an inkstand without ink, and a few pens parched by long disuse. The place seemed fitted for quiet study and profound meditation. It was buried deep among the massive walls of the abbey, and shut up from the tumult of the world.

I had taken down a little thick quarto, curiously bound in parchment, with brass clasps, and seated myself at the table in a venerable elbow-chair. Instead of reading, however, I was beguiled by the solemn monastic air, and lifeless quiet of the place, into a train of musing. As I looked around upon the old volumes in their mouldering covers, thus ranged on the shelves, and apparently never disturbed in their repose, I could not but consider the library a kind of literary catacomb, where authors, like mummies, are piously entombed, and left to blacken and moulder in dusty oblivion.

How much, thought I, has each of these volumes, now thrust aside with such indifference, cost some aching head! how many weary days! how many sleepless nights! How have their authors buried themselves in the solitude of cells and cloisters; shut themselves up from the face of man, and the still more blessed face of nature; and devoted themselves to painful research and intense reflection! And all for what? to occupy an inch of dusty shelf—to have the title of their works read now and then in a future age, by some drowsy churchman or casual straggler like myself; and in another age to be lost, even to remembrance.

Source: "The Mutability of Literature" from *The Sketchbook of Geoffrey Crayon* by Washington Irving

18. The reference to the library as "a kind of literary catacomb" serves to:
    (a) describe the decay of old, unread books.
    (b) show that the work of many authors is without purpose.
    (c) introduce the reader to the setting of the essay.
    (d) compare the quiet of the library to that of a tomb.
    (e) illustrate how a library is a figurative cemetery for authors of old, unread books.

19. Which of the following is **suggested** by the author?
    (a) Writing is often a solitary pursuit.
    (b) The library at Westminster Abbey is used by the Westminster School.
    (c) Air castles are best built in libraries.
    (d) Overuse is the biggest enemy of library books.
    (e) The library at Westminster Abbey is in the basement.

20. The **main** idea of the passage is:
    (a) literature can experience a kind of death.
    (b) there are too many books for society to continue to read them all.
    (c) libraries can be the death of books.
    (d) too much time to think can lead one to morbid conclusions.
    (e) many writers waste their time pursuing their art.

21. All of these are assertions of opinion **except:**
    (a) Writers must devote themselves to painful research and intense reflection.
    (b) The roof of the library is supported by massive joists of old English oak.
    (c) The inkstand is empty because the ink dried up over the course of many years without use.
    (d) Old books by polemical writers are read rarely, and then only by drowsy churchmen or casual stragglers.
    (e) To be able to enter a state of reflection, one should remove oneself from noise and other distractions.

VII The Life and Work of Michael Faraday

Often referred to as Britain's greatest experimental scientist, Michael Faraday had an unpromising start. He had to leave school at the age of thirteen to work as an apprentice to a bookbinder. He spent eight years in this employment, during which time he read many of the books he bound. The young Faraday was particularly interested in scientific writings. He revealed later in a letter to a friend: "There were two that especially helped me, the *Encyclopaedia Britannica* from which I gained my first notions of electricity and Mrs. Marcet's Conversation on Chemistry, which gave me foundation in that science...[F]acts were important to me, and saved me. I could trust a fact, and always cross-examine an assertion."

In 1812, Faraday attended 4 lectures given by Sir Humphry Davy, a chemist at the Royal Institution. Enthralled, he took careful notes, which he copied and bound. These lectures inspired Faraday to attempt to leave the bookbinding profession and enter the field of science. He wrote to the President of the Royal Society, Sir Joseph Banks, to ask for advice. Banks never replied, but Faraday remained resolute. He wrote to Davy, presenting him with a copy of his lecture notes.

Davy was so impressed with Faraday that, a few months later, he recommended him for an assistant position. Faraday soon became Assistant and Superintendent of the Apparatus of the Laboratory and Mineral Collection. He worked with Davy on inventions such as the safe mining lamp, and conducted his own research, performing experiments with electromagnetic rotations. In 1821, he became Superintendent of the house and laboratory, and began publishing his work.

Many historians believe that Davy became jealous of his assistant, and deliberately tried to stymie his career. Until his death in 1829, Davy assigned Faraday many lengthy experiments that always proved fruitless. For example, Faraday worked for six years on optical glass experiments, achieving nothing. When Faraday was nominated for the Royal Society, Davy objected. However, he was elected in 1824 and became director of the laboratory at the Royal Institute a year later.

Although Faraday made many important discoveries in both chemistry and physics, he is best known for his understanding of electromagnetism. The discovery that electricity could be made by moving a magnet inside a wire coil led to the invention of the electric motor, which in turn transformed society. Many of the words used today to discuss electricity, including ion, electrode, cathode and anode, were first used by Faraday.

Despite his reputation as one of the greatest scientific experimentalists of all time, Faraday enjoyed speaking with young people and explaining, in terms they could understand, topics such as "the nature of water," and "air necessary for combustion." Considered a classic of science literature, The Chemical History of the Candle, was originally a series of children's lectures delivered by Faraday at the Royal Institution. His apparent ease with distilling science to make it palatable and interesting to his young audience is remarkable, because the nature of his experimentation and theorizing was highly technical. In fact, his scientific discoveries, including that of magneto-electric induction, cannot even be adequately described or understood without rigorous study of chemistry and physics.

22. What is the **main** idea of the passage?

    (a) Those who overcome difficult situations in childhood often attain great success in adulthood.

    (b) Michael Faraday's invention of the electric motor changed society.

    (c) Scientist Michael Faraday is remarkable not only for his success, but also for his perseverance.

    (d) The partnership between Michael Faraday and Humphry Davy produced many important scientific theories.

    (e) Although Faraday delivered it as a lecture, The Chemical History of the Candle was published and became a classic of science literature.

23. Which of the following **cannot** be inferred from the passage?

    (a) The relationship between Faraday and Sir Humphry Davy deteriorated.

    (b) Faraday did not speak to lecture audiences in the way he wrote his papers.

    (c) Faraday became interested in electricity while working as a bookbinder.

    (d) Sir Joseph Banks did not encourage Faraday to enter the field of science.

    (e) Faraday gained no useful education while working as a bookbinder.

24. Which of the following is a statement of **fact** rather than an assertion of opinion?

    (a) Faraday disliked the experiments assigned to him by Davy.

    (b) Faraday was able to conduct his own research while working as Assistant and Superintendent of the Apparatus of the Laboratory and Mineral Collection.

    (c) Faraday was disappointed when he got no reply from Sir Joseph Banks to his letter.

    (d) Davy became jealous of Faraday and tried to stymie his career.

    (e) Faraday enjoyed speaking to young people because it allowed him to describe his work in terms that could be easily understood.

VIII Aphra Behn and Restoration Comedy

When the monarchy was restored in 1660, Charles II was summoned to the throne from exile in France. His ensuing 25-year reign was marked by the Great Plague, the Fire of London, political conspiracies, religious persecution and massive royal debt. However, Charles was also responsible for reopening England's theatres, which had been closed in 1642 by the Puritans. While his interest in the theatre may have been a byproduct of the influence of his mistress, actress Nell Gwyn, it led to a national revitalization in the dramatic arts.

We now refer to the humorous plays written and performed during this era as Restoration Comedies. They were a radical departure from the dramas their audience remembered from two decades earlier, with their penchant for the burlesque and sharp-witted repartee. For the first time, women performed on stage, abolishing the once standard casting of men and boys in female parts.

Appreciative audiences made celebrities of many actresses, whose parts were written specifically to get them entangled in suggestive situations. At least a quarter of the comedies of the period had a "breeches role," in which an actress would disguise herself as a boy or man in order to deceive one or more of the other characters. At that time women's bodies were normally hidden by long and voluminous skirts, so the display of the female figure in tight-fitting pants was a novelty appreciated by predominantly male theatregoers.

Innovation in the theatre did not stop with the plays themselves. The Restoration produced England's first woman playwright, Aphra Behn, who was also the first professional woman writer in Britain. Behn was one of the most prolific dramatists of the time, writing and producing at least 16 plays between 1670 and 1689. Her works, like those of her contemporaries, were often about sexual intrigue, and their bawdy nature rivaled that of the works of Behn's male contemporaries.

Although her plays were highly successful, many reviled them (along with other Restoration Comedies) for their perceived indecency. Three hundred years after her death, an anonymous writer mused: "Mrs. Behn is still to be found here and there in the dusty, worm-eaten libraries of old country houses, but, as a rule, we imagine, she has been ejected from all decent society for more than a generation or two. If Mrs. Behn is to be read at all, it can only be from a love of impurity for its own sake[...]. It is true that [her scandalous reputation] did not prohibit her from attaining honourable burial in Westminster Abbey, but it is a pity her books did not rot with her bones."

If a consensus regarding the content of her plays was impossible, there is no dispute that Behn was a master of staging. The visual element of her work was not an afterthought, as it was for many of her contemporaries, but an integral part of the play. She is recognised as the inventor of what is now referred to as the discovery scene, in which stage devices such as trap doors and moving scenery helped to develop the plot.

25. What is the **main** purpose of the last paragraph?

    (a) to illustrate why Behn's reputation as a playwright is in flux

    (b) to demonstrate how breeches roles worked in Behn's plays

    (c) to give an example of Behn's contributions to drama

    (d) to highlight the role of women in the Restoration Comedy

    (e) to explain why Behn was a favourite of Charles II

26. With which of the following would the author of the passage most likely **agree**?

    (a) Aphra Behn was the most prolific playwright of the Restoration period.

    (b) The reign of Charles II was marked by innovations in the dramatic arts.

    (c) Behn's plays were influenced by the work of English women writers.

    (d) Breeches roles allowed women to engage in the witty repartee that was a hallmark of Restoration Comedy.

    (e) Behn's detractors preferred the drama of the pre-Restoration era to Restoration Comedy.

IX Sushi

Sushi started small in the United States, in a handful of restaurants in big cities. But it caught on. Today, sushi consumption in American restaurants is 40% greater than it was in the late 1990's, according to the National Restaurant Association. The concession stands at almost every major league stadium sell sushi, and many colleges and universities offer it in their dining halls. But Americans are not just eating it out. The National Sushi Association reports that there are over 5,000 sushi bars in supermarkets, and that number is growing monthly. Increases in availability and consumption point to the fact that Americans have decided sushi isn't just good for them, or simply convenient, but the once-scorned food is truly delicious.

The origins of this hot food trend may be found in Asia, where it was developed as a way of preserving fish. Fresh, cleaned fish was pressed between rice and salt and weighted with a heavy stone over a period of several months. During this time, the rice fermented, producing lactic acid that pickled and preserved the fish. For many years, the fish was eaten and the rice was discarded. But about 500 years ago, that changed, and hako-zushi (boxed sushi) was created. In this type of sushi, the rice and fish are pressed together in a box and are meant to be consumed together.

In 1824, Yohei Hanaya of Edo (now called Tokyo) eliminated the fermentation process, and began serving fresh slices of seafood on bases of vinegared rice. The vinegar was probably used to mimic the taste of fermented sushi. In fact, the word "sushi" actually refers to any vinegared rice dish, and not to the fish, as many Americans believe (the fish is called sashimi). In Japanese, when "sushi" is combined with a modifier, it changes to the word "zushi."

Japanese chef Yohei's invention, called nigiri zushi, is still served today. It now refers to a slice of fish (cooked or uncooked) that is pressed by hand onto a serving of rice. Popular choices include ama ebi (Japanese for raw shrimp), shime saba (marinated mackerel), and shime ebi (marinated shrimp). In addition to the vinegar flavor in the rice, nigiri zushi typically contains a taste of horseradish (wasabi), and is served with soy sauce for dipping.

Maki zushi contains strips of fish or vegetables rolled in rice and wrapped in thin sheets of nori, or dried seaweed. Popular ingredients include smoked salmon, fresh crab, shrimp, octopus, raw clams, and sea urchin. Americans have invented many of their own maki zushi combinations, including the California roll, which contains imitation crab meat and avocado. They have also made innovations in the construction of maki zushi. Some American sushi bars switch the placement of nori and rice, while others don't use nori, and instead roll the maki zushi in fish roe. These colorful, crunchy eggs add to the visual and taste appeal of the dish.

27. Which of the following is **not** stated in the passage?
    (a) Wasabi is typically an ingredient of nigiri zushi.
    (b) The rice in hako-zushi is meant to be consumed with the fish.
    (c) Sushi was developed as a method for preserving fish.
    (d) Lactic acid, produced by fermenting rice, preserves fish.
    (e) Tokyo is the capital of Japan and was once known as Edo.

28. Which of the following may be **inferred** from the passage?
    (a) Many Americans believe the word sushi refers to fish.
    (b) The most popular ingredient of maki zushi is fresh crab.
    (c) Ebi is the Japanese word for shrimp.
    (d) Every month more sushi bars open in supermarkets.
    (e) Maki zushi is sometimes rolled in roe, which is also known as dried seaweed.

X The Compact Disc

Compact discs (CDs), which may be found in over 80% of British homes, not to mention backpacks and automobiles, first entered popular culture in the 1980s. But their history goes back to the 1960's, when an inventor named James Russell decided to create an alternative to his scratched and warped phonograph records--a system that could record, store, and replay music without ever wearing out.

Russell knew that this could only be accomplished if the various parts of the system did not come into physical contact with one another; the music would instead be read optically. The result was the compact disc (CD). Made from 1.2 mm of polycarbonate plastic, the disk is coated with a much thinner aluminum layer that is then protected with a film of lacquer. The lacquer layer can be printed with a label. CDs are typically 120 mm in diameter and can store about 74 minutes of music. There are also discs that can store 80, 90, 99, and 100 minutes of music, but they are not as compatible with various stereos and computers as the 74-minute size.

The information on a standard CD is contained on the polycarbonate layer, as a single spiral track of pits, starting at the inside of the disk and circling its way to the outside. The pits look like bumps to the player because the CD is read through the bottom of the disc. Areas without pits are known as land. The player distinguished bumps from land by the light that is reflected (or not reflected) off the aluminum—pits produce no reflection, while land does.

This process is accomplished by a 780 mm wavelength semiconductor laser, which is shone through the bottom of the polycarbonate layer. Once the laser "reads" the tracks of bumps and land, the changes in reflectivity are interpreted by a part of the compact disk player known as the detector. It is the job of the detector to convert the information collected by the laser into the music that was originally recorded onto the disk.

In the 1970s, a number of companies, including Sony and Phillips, bought licenses for the technology and began working on the disks. By 1979, Sony and Phillips joined forces, with Sony contributing the error-correction method, or CIRC, and Phillips contributing the general manufacturing process. Further advances with the technology brought the CD-ROM, and the CD-R, which, together with audio CD, had 2004 worldwide sales of over 30 billion discs.

29. All of the following are shown in the passage **except:**

    (a) CDs are read optically.

    (b) The detector converts a CD's pattern of reflections into music.

    (c) There are a number of reasons for the popularity of the 120mm disc.

    (d) Russell's invention began as frustration with his record albums.

    (e) Licenses for Russell's CD technology were sold.

30. The **purpose** of paragraph four can best be described as:

    (a) to introduce all of the parts of a CD player

    (b) to explain how the music stored on a CD is read

    (c) to show how Russell's optical system preserves CDs

    (d) to examine the role of the laser in CD technology

    (e) to explain how the detector works

SECTION B: ESSAY

Answer ONE of the following questions.

Your response should be a reasoned and substantiated argument which justifies your response to the question. You may use one sheet of paper for planning your essay. Your essay must be no longer than 4 pages.

1. Downloading music for free is a form of stealing. Do you agree?
2. Professional athletes should be barred from participating in the Olympics. Do you agree?
3. Extraordinary measures are justified in order to protect endangered species from extinction. How do you respond to this statement?
4. The public's fascination with celebrity culture is a dangerous social trend. How do you respond to this statement?
5. Should the use of performance-enhancing substitutes such as steroids be tolerated in the world of professional athletics? How do you respond to this question?

ANSWERS AND EXPLANATIONS

Answer Key

1. (e)	9. (c)	17. (c)	25. (c)
2. (d)	10. (e)	18. (e)	26. (b)
3. (a)	11. (a)	19. (a)	27. (e)
4. (c)	12. (b)	20. (a)	28. (c)
5. (a)	13. (d)	21. (b)	29. (c)
6. (b)	14. (a)	22. (c)	30. (b)
7. (d)	15. (d)	23. (e)	
8. (d)	16. (e)	24. (b)	

1. (e)

The paragraph gives a picture of Gergiev. It tells the reader that he is one of the world's best-known conductors, that he works in a baseball cap, that he answers difficult interview questions with ease, and doesn't get fazed when fireworks disrupt his performance. Both sentences centre on the conductor, and serve no other purpose but to introduce him to the reader.

(a) The only mention of Vladimir Putin is in the last paragraph. There is no statement or suggestion in the first paragraph or anywhere else in the passage regarding Gergiev's opinion of the Russian President.

(b) The expansion of the Hermitage is mentioned only in paragraph four.

(c) The paragraph states that Gergiev is not made uncomfortable by questions about "the ascendancy of his opera and ballet company, the Mariinsky, over the Bolshoi," but give no reasons for the ascendancy. Paragraphs four and five give possible reasons.

(d) While it is stated that fireworks disrupted the concert, this answer choice is too specific and limited to be the purpose of the paragraph.

2. (d)

This question asks you to differentiate between facts stated in the article and opinions postulated. All five answer choices can be found in the article, but only one will be objectively true. Choice **(d)** is a fact found in the second paragraph. A person's ethnicity and geographic point of origin are factually verifiable and, therefore, not assertions. Keep in mind that this question type is relatively easy: find the answer choice that sounds like a fact rather than an opinion.

Choices **(a)**, **(b)**, and **(c)** cannot be verified. They are statements of opinion rather than fact. Although eventually it will be determined whether **(e)** is true, at the time of writing the article, the statement is a rumour, not a fact.

3. (a)

This is a logic question. To answer it, one must first identify the argument made by the author, and then determine which answer would weaken that argument. In this case, what is meant by the assertion: "The two institutions' other edge is St Petersburg itself"? A careful reading of the paragraph reveals the author's argument: St Petersburg is helpful to or positive for the Mariinsky and the Hermitage. Four answer choices strengthen the argument, or are irrelevant to it. Only one, **(a)**, correctly weakens the argument. If St Petersburg is an ugly industrial town, it is no better than Moscow, and therefore not an "edge."

(b) and **(c)** are stated by the author in the paragraph in support of the argument. They strengthen rather than weaken it.

(d) is irrelevant. The reputation of the former prime minister has nothing to do with the positive impact of St Petersburg on the Mariinsky and the Hermitage.

(e) may be inferred, not only because of the presence of the Mariinsky and the Hermitage, but also because the author describes Moscow as an ugly city. More tourists mean more business, so this statement also strengthens the author's argument.

4. (c)

This question asks you to find the one statement that is not stated or implicit in statements made in the passage. The paragraph about Daimler's acquisition of Chrysler states that Daimler had a high cost base that it hoped to lower though the acquisition. Choice **(c)**, which states the opposite, is therefore the correct choice.

Choices **(a)**, **(b)**, **(d)**, and **(e)** are incorrect because they can be found in or inferred from the article. In the first paragraph we learn that the ten largest manufacturers produce over 58 brands (so more than four dozen). Chart 2 shows Renault's higher operating margin percentage. Paragraph three explains that Ford's takeover of a number of brands, including Jaguar, has not increased its profitability. The alliance of Renault and Nissan occurred a year after the takeover of Chrysler by Daimler-Benz in 1998.

5. (a)

This question asks you to select the only answer choice referred to in the article that seems likely to succeed in increasing profitability. The author describes how the quality of Mercedes slipped while the company was busy improving Chrysler. The slip in quality resulted directly in Mercedes losing "its long-standing dominance of the lucrative German market to its arch-rival BMW." Losing dominance in a lucrative market is clearly not a method for increasing profitability, so presumably maintaining quality will tend to have the opposite effect.

(b) is mentioned in paragraph five as one of the reasons Daimler took over Chrysler. However, while in theory the spreading out of cost over a bigger output may make sense, the article states that it did not increase profitability for Daimler.

(c) is incorrect since the point of the entire passage is that auto industry acquisition failed to bring success to the acquirers and thus the consolidation trend is becoming "extinct."

(d) and **(e)** are incorrect, since according to the fourth paragraph Chrysler was "licked into shape" (made more profitable) by slashing surplus capacity and creating good new products.

6. (b)

This question asks you to identify the author's reason for using the charts. The charts show that the manufacturer at the top of the first chart (the one with the most brands) is nearly at the bottom of the second chart (one of the least profitable). In addition, the quote in choice **(b)** is the topic sentence of the second paragraph, which ends with a parenthetical "see the charts."

(a) is too specific. The charts are about the manufacturers, their brands, and their profitability. Conclusions are drawn about more than one of those manfacturers from the charts. The article does not focus on DaimlerChrysler alone.

(c) is wrong for two reasons. First, it centres only on the second chart, but even that chart is not included to "demonstrate the need" for profitability. Second, the author does not need to explain why a company needs to be profitable.

(d) is untrue. The first paragraph states that most manufacturers retain brands (or "badges") after consolidation.

(e) mentions global vehicle production, which is not dealt with in the article.

7. (d)

This is an inference question asking you to identify the choice that must be true based on the information in the article. Wrong choices will either be untrue or overtly stated (meaning they did not have to be inferred). The article states that GM's purchase of other companies has not made it successful, so you may infer that, as a company in business to make money, GM will attempt to increase its profitability through other means.

(a) This choice is incorrect because it is stated clearly in the fourth paragraph.

(b) The first chart shows that Honda produced about 3 million cars, compared with VW's 5 million.

(c) The second paragraph compares the charts, noting that although Chrysler has the most brands, it is second to last in the "profitability league."

(e) You do not need to make an inference with this choice, because it is clearly stated in the last paragraph: Jürgen Schrempp "was nudged out of his chief executive's chair…as a result" of the failed merger.

8. **(d)**

The author describes the difficulties of writing about landscape, including three of its "persistent enemies." Choice **(d)** generally encompasses the ideas presented in the passage without getting too specific.

(a) and **(c)** are not mentioned in the passage. Paragraph three states that British writers are increasingly avoiding the subject of landscape, but not that they ***should*** do so. In paragraph four, the author makes a connection between the decline of landscape writing and modern literature's exploration of the subject of alienation, but never states that there is no place for landscape writing in modern literature.

(e) is, according to the passage, true for some writers. However, it is just one of the many ideas presented in the passage. It is too specific and limiting to be the main idea.

9. **(c)**

This question asks you to select the one answer choice that is not implied in the passage. The other four choices can be assumed to be true, even though they have not been explicitly stated. Choice **(c)** is correct because the author never states or implies a connection between landscape and politics. Instead, he describes in the last paragraph the negative effects of "an infatuation with the landscape," rather than the landscape itself.

(a) is incorrect. From the sentence "Rose Tremain reported recently that she had taken to setting her novels either abroad or in the past, because there was 'no immediate landscape left with which to engage' in contemporary Britain" we can infer that she would prefer 1840 (in the past) to 2005 (contemporary Britain).

The author notes the difficulty of making landscape writing original by calling it a cliché and the "canning-factory of style." He urges the reader to try coming up with a landscape description that is unique.

(b) can be inferred from the article, making it incorrect.

(d) is implied by the argument in paragraph four. If landscape writing is "pensionable," it isn't employed by writers seeking to explore "peculiarly modern sentiments."

(e) is implied by the argument in the second paragraph. The author notes that overuse of landscape writing has layered years of "dead language" on it, making it "effortful work to get back through the verbal crud" to fresh landscape writing.

10. (e)

The key to answering this question correctly is focusing on context. There are a number of clues within paragraph six that effectively define the term. The first is the mention of over-writing as a problem with landscape writing. In addition, "effusion" and "excessively adjectival loquacity" are used to develop the idea of over-writing. Even if you aren't sure of the meaning of loquacity, you should recognise "excessive" and "adjective." If over-writing is bad, then "more words will always be better than fewer" (used as an example of pleonastic heresy) must also be a problem. Using more words when a few will do means being redundant, which points to choice **(e)**.

Choices **(a)**, **(b)**, and **(d)** all contain words that mean the opposite of pleonastic (or excessive, effusive, or over-written). "Lean," "terse," and "concise" therefore make these choices incorrect. Choice **(c)** uses a synonym for pleonastic (loquacious), a form of which appears in the paragraph, but "misconception" is not synonymous with heresy.

11. (a)

This question requires you to locate the answer choice that is not a supported fact but rather an opinion or unsupported statement. The four wrong choices are facts that can be proven to be true. Choice **(a)** is not factually verifiable, but rather an opinion, making it an assertion.

12. (b)

Researcher bias is mentioned in the last three paragraphs, twice as part of conclusions drawn by Dr. Ioannidis. We can assume that he would agree with choice **(b)**.

(a) is incorrect since paragraph four paraphrases Dr Ioannidis: "many seemingly meaningful results are bound to be wrong just by chance".

(c) and **(d)** are antithetical to Dr Ioannidis' research and viewpoint. **(c)** refutes his thesis as it is explained in the article, which explicitly states that he believes less than 50% of all studies' conclusions are correct. Paragraph three's discussion of conclusions that were later disproven mentions the opposite of **(d)**. In paragraph four, Dr Ioannidis's belief that "unsophisticated reliance on statistical significance" is a major factor in the poor quality of scientific studies.

(e) is specifically refuted in the last sentence.

13. (d)

This question asks you to find the only answer choice that is not mentioned as a factor that contributes to false results in a scientific study. Choices **(a)**, **(b)**, **(c)**, and **(e)** are all mentioned in paragraphs four and five as such factors. But there is nothing in the article to suggest **(d)**—that the amount of time spent (or not spent) on a study is a factor contributing to false results.

14. (a)

This question asks you to find the one statement that cannot be gathered from the article. Choice **(a)** is correct because the author clearly states in paragraph 1 that Cellini's autobiography "takes its place" among the other autobiographies he cites. There is nothing in the passage to suggest that Symonds finds Cellini's work superior to the others.

(b) may be inferred, making it incorrect. Paragraph three states that Cellini gives "only glimpses" of great events and people such as the Pope and the Emperor, and paragraph four notes that there is a much more complete picture of the "artistic life of the time."

(c) and **(e)** are inferences drawn on these references, so they are incorrect. There are references to Cellini's boastful nature in paragraphs two and five. Symonds says Cellini wrote his autobiography so the world would know about the great things he did. He also refers to him as a braggart who had a "keen interest" in himself.

(d) may also be inferred from the passage. Symonds notes that out of all the autobiographies written, only three or four are great. One may therefore conclude that he believes most of them to be ordinary, or even inferior.

15. (d)

This question asks you to make an inference based on material found in the passage. At the beginning of the paragraph, Symonds describes first Cellini's character ("a murderer and a braggart, insolent, sensual, inordinately proud and passionate"), and then describes his work in gold and silver. At the end of the paragraph, he notes that Cellini is better known for his autobiography than for his "Perseus" or his goldsmithing. One may therefore infer that the reference to Perseus has something to do with Cellini's character.

You could also use the process of elimination to arrive at the correct answer. There is nothing in the passage to suggest that Cellini studied Greek mythology, or that he had a pet. Choices **(a)** and **(c)** are both incorrect. Similarly, the Cellini family's origins are not discussed, making **(b)** incorrect. Although Cellini's friendship with Michelangelo is mentioned in paragraph four, specific works by the artist, and his use of his friend as a model, are not mentioned. **(e)** is also incorrect.

16. (e)

The right answer is the only one that is not stated in the passage. Although the statement in **(e)** might be true, it is not stated in the passage. Paragraph five states that Cellini was a murderer, but there is no information about any punishment or lack thereof.

(a) In the first paragraph Symonds mentions Rousseau's "Confessions" as one of the four masterpieces of the genre.

(b) "The scene is mainly in Italy and France," according to paragraph three.

(c) According to paragraph four, "Michelangelo himself he knew and adored."

(d) Paragraph two says, "Pepys noted down in his diary the daily events of his life for his sole satisfaction and with no intention that any one should read the cipher in which they were recorded."

17. (c)

The author places Cellini's work in the company of four better-known, highly esteemed autobiographical works. Symonds also explains that Cellini gives a view of the artistic and social life of Italy during the Renaissance. It may be inferred that his goal is to show that Cellini's autobiography is important and that it deserves an audience. Therefore choice **(c)** is correct.

(a) is incorrect, since the source of the passage reveals that Symonds translated Cellini's autobiography, and that the passage is from the introduction he wrote to that work. However, while it is possible that Symonds would use the introduction to explain the translation process, there is no mention of this work.

(b) is incorrect. The information about sixteenth century Italy in the passage is highlights from Cellini's work. There is no indication that it is included to give the reader context.

(d) is incorrect since Symonds does note that Cellini was a sensual, insolent murderer, but he never makes excuses for this behaviour.

(e) is incorrect. The beginning of the passage places Cellini's work in the company of three other "masterpieces" of autobiography, and explains the differences in intention between the four authors. However, Symonds does not make claims about autobiography's status relative to other forms of literature.

18. (e)

This question asks you to select the answer choice that explains the metaphor comparing the library to a catacomb. Authors are described as being "like mummies," which should lead you to choice **(e)**.

(a) is too specific to encompass the entire meaning of the image of the library as a catacomb, which does include the physical decay ("blacken" and "moulder") of the books, but goes on further to explain that the authors are "piously entombed."

(b) is incorrect since the last paragraph, and not the image of the library as a catacomb, explores the idea that many authors labour over their work, only to be "lost, even to remembrance."

(c) is incorrect because the setting, the library in Westminster Abbey, is introduced in paragraphs one and two.

(d) is incorrect because the image is not about sound.

19. (a)

This is an inference question. You must identify the choice that must be true, based on the information in the passage. In the last paragraph, Irving describes writers who "buried themselves in the solitude of cells and cloisters; shut themselves up from the face of man, and the still more blessed face of nature."

(b) is incorrect, since there is no evidence in the passage that the school used the library. We can assume, however, that the dusty condition of the library indicates that it is rarely used, especially by "madcap boys."

(c) states Irving is in the library. He mentions the building of air castles once, in the first paragraph, where he is "loitering about the old gray cloisters of Westminster Abbey.

(d) is incorrect. In paragraph two, the author describes books that "were much more worn by time than use." You may infer that time is an enemy to library books, perhaps as much or more so than overuse (which is not mentioned in the passage).

(e) is not correct because Irving describes the library as a "lofty antique hall, the roof supported by massive joists of old English oak." Basements are not described as lofty, and one cannot see the joists that support a roof from a basement.

20. (a)

Remember that incorrect answers to main idea questions are typically either too specific, or draw conclusions that can't be supported by the passage. Choice **(a)** is correct because throughout the passage, Irving uses images that support it, personifying the books and describing their lifelessness. The library and the books within are described as removed from the real world, "buried deep," "shut up from the tumult of the world." In the "lifeless quiet" it appears that the books were "never disturbed in their repose." We have already looked at the image of the catacomb where authors are entombed in "dusty oblivion."

(b) is incorrect because it cannot be supported by anything in the passage.

(c) is a mischaracterization of Irving's image. He does suggest that books can "die," but the library does not commit the "murder." Rather, the library is merely the tomb in which the "dead" books rest.

(d) is too specific to be the main idea. Irving does describe his pensive mood a number of times in the passage, but there is much more to the passage that cannot be summed up by this choice.

(e) is also too specific to be the main idea. The last paragraph explains the difficult work of the writer whose work can be "thrust aside with such indifference" and be "lost, even to remembrance."

21. (b)

This assertion question asks you to differentiate between facts stated in the article and opinions postulated. All five answer choices can be found in the article, but only one will be objectively true. Choice **(b)** is a description, which can sometimes be subjective. However in this case it is objective. Irving is merely reporting what he has observed. One could, in fact, visit the library and prove it to be true.

There is no way to verify choice **(a)**, so it is an assertion. Note the use of adjectives that create a subjective picture. Perhaps one could verify that authors must do research, but when that research is described as "painful," it moves from fact to assertion. Irving does note that the inkstand is empty, but there is no way to know if the ink was used up and never replaced, or if it dried up over time. Therefore **(c)** is incorrect. Again, the subjective detail that such books are only read by "drowsy churchmen" and "causal stragglers" make choice **(d)** an unverifiable statement. While choice **(e)** may be true for Irving, one cannot verify how a state of reflection is entered into. Experiences of mental states are subjective, and therefore assertions.

22. (c)

The wrong answer choices in main idea questions usually fall into one of three categories: they are too specific to encompass the theme of the passage, they draw an incorrect conclusion, or they are beyond the scope of the passage. Choice **(c)** best describes the passage as a whole. The passage notes that Faraday studied science on his own, took notes at Davy's lecture, wrote to two prominent scientists asking for advice and performed his own experiments while working for a jealous supervisor. These facts can be paraphrased by the word "perseverance."

(a) is general enough to be a main idea, but it is incorrect because the passage does not include a discussion of other successful people. There is no basis for this conclusion.

Conversely, **(b)**, **(d)**, and **(e)** are too specific. The author notes that Faraday's invention changed society and that the lecture series became a classic, but these are details, not main ideas. While Faraday and Davy did work together, this is not only a detail, but it is also incorrectly described as a "partnership." Faraday worked under Davy.

23. (e)

Inferences are conclusions that must be true based on the information provided in the article. They are not directly stated in the passage. You are looking for the one choice that ***cannot*** be inferred, so the other choices ***can*** be inferred. Choice **(e)** is correct—it cannot be inferred, because we are told in the first paragraph that, while working as a bookbinder was an "unpromising" start, Faraday read many of the books he worked on, and two in particular are cited as influencing his future work.

(a) is incorrect. One can conclude that if Davy was once so impressed by Faraday that he helped him get a job, but later became jealous of Faraday, their relationship changed for the worse.

(b) is incorrect since the last paragraph states that Faraday lectured to young people, "distilling science to make it palatable and interesting" to them. Since his work is described as "highly technical," it may be inferred that his lectures did not sound like his scientific papers.

(c) is incorrect. In the first paragraph, there is a quote from one of Faraday's letters written while he worked as a bookbinder. He describes his fondness for the ***Encyclopaedia Britannica*** from which he first learned about electricity. Since he was obviously exposed to a wide range of reading topics, and singled out electricity, we can infer that it was an interest of his.

(d) is incorrect. The author writes that Faraday sent a letter to Banks, but Banks never replied. We may therefore infer that Banks did not encourage Faraday.

24. (b)

The correct answer must be objectively true. Paragraph three states that Faraday "became Assistant and Superintendent of the Apparatus of the Laboratory and Mineral Collection" where he "worked with Davy on inventions such as the safe mining lamp, and conducted his own research."

(a) Faraday's feelings toward the mostly fruitless experiments assigned to him by Davy are not known, although it may be inferred that he disliked them.

(c) It is a fact that Faraday received no reply to his letter, but his reaction to that fact is unknown and simply an opinion.

(d) Although many historians ***believe*** it to be true, Davy's jealousy and deliberate interference in Faraday's career are conjecture, not facts.

(e) The passage states both that Faraday enjoyed speaking to young people and that in his talks he described his work in terms that could be easily understood. However, there is no causal relationship between the two; it is not a fact that he enjoyed speaking to young people ***because*** of how it allowed him to describe his work.

25. (c)

This question asks you to identify the role of the last paragraph in the writer's overall purpose. The paragraph's topic sentence is the first one: "...there is no dispute that Behn was a master of staging." It goes on to explain why she was a master, acknowledging her emphasis on the visual element of drama, and her invention of the discovery scene. This may be summarised as a contribution to drama, making choice **(c)** the correct one.

(a) Although Behn's detractors and their arguments are mentioned, there is nothing in the paragraph to explain *why* her reputation fluctuated, or even to suggest that those who agree she is a master of staging still find her content disagreeable.

(b) Breeches roles were a visual element of Restoration Comedy, but the last paragraph does not demonstrate how they worked in Behn's plays.

(d) The paragraph is about a particular contribution made by Behn, and not the general role of women. This answer choice is too vague, as the role of women could refer to actresses, the parts they played, or female playwrights such as Behn.

(e) The passage never states or implies that Charles II was a fan of Behn's work.

26. (b)

The passage explains that women were first allowed to act onstage during Charles II's reign, and that the period saw the emergence of the first professional woman writer, the successful playwright Aphra Behn. These innovations make **(b)** the correct answer.

(a) is incorrect. Paragraph four states that Behn was "one of the most" prolific playwrights of the period, not "the most" prolific.

(c) is incorrect since Behn was "England's first woman playwright," there were no past examples to rely upon.

(d) is incorrect because there is nothing in the passage to suggest that actresses could not engage in witty repartee unless they were playing a breeches role. There is no logical connection between the type of dialogue and the role.

(e) is incorrect. Behn's detractors disliked the perceived indecency of her plays, but there is no reason to believe they preferred earlier drama. In fact, they may have viewed the stage in general as negatively as any specific type of production.

27. (e)

Remember that in this statement question, the correct answer must **not** be explicitly stated in the passage. It could be an inference or a true statement that doesn't appear in the passage. Choice **(e)** is correct because although Tokyo is the capital of Japan, that fact is not stated in the passage.

(a) The last sentence of paragraph four states that "nigiri zushi typically contains a taste of horseradish (wasabi)."

(b) The description of hako-zuski in the second paragraph states "the rice and fish are pressed together in a box, and are meant to be consumed together."

(c) and **(d)** The second paragraph states that sushi was developed as a way of preserving fish, and that the preservation occurs when the rice ferments.

28. (c)

This is a type of inference question. You are looking for an answer that must be true based on the information in the passage. Choice **(c)** is correct because if ama ebi is Japanese for raw shrimp and shime ebi is Japanese for marinated shrimp, you may gather that the Japanese word for shrimp is ebi.

(a) is stated in the second paragraph ("the word 'sushi' actually refers to any vinegared rice dish, and not to the fish, as many Americans believe").

(b) and **(e)** are incorrect because they are not true according to the passage. Paragraph five says that fresh crab is *one of* the popular ingredients, not *the* most popular. That paragraph also notes that nori is dried seaweed. Fish roe is "colourful, crunchy eggs."

(d) is incorrect. In the first paragraph we learn that "there are over 5,000 sushi bars in supermarkets, and that number is growing monthly."

29. (c)

This question asks you to locate the information that does not appear in the passage. Choice **(c)** is correct because only one reason, size compatibility, is mentioned. The other four answer choices may all be found in the text.

30. (b)

The correct answer must be general enough to encompass all of the information contained in the paragraph, and specific enough to refer only to that paragraph (not to information discussed elsewhere in the passage).

(a) is incorrect because only two parts, the laser and the detector, are mentioned.

(c) is wrong since the paragraph does show how the CD is read optically by a laser, but its overall purpose is not about the preservation of the CD.

(d) and **(e)** are too limiting; the laser and detector are both mentioned, but neither subject is broad enough to encompass the purpose of the paragraph.

Essay Responses

1. Downloading music for free is a form of stealing. Do you agree?

Stealing can simply be defined as taking something that belongs to someone else without that person's permission. When we consider if downloading music for free is stealing we must consider to whom does music belong. Does it belong to the purchaser of a CD—as advocates for unrestricted file sharing might have us believe—or does it belong to the person who created the music, either the songwriter or the recording artist? Copyright law is quite clear on this point. Music, like any other creative work, is the property of the creators unless they have signed over their rights to some third party. Therefore, we must agree that taking a song without compensating the artist who created the work is taking something that belongs to someone else, that is, stealing.

So why is this issue so controversial? The term 'file sharing' belies the mistaken notion that allows some people to believe that downloading music for free is not stealing. Those who argue that users should be allowed to download music without compensating the artist suggest that it is form of acceptable 'sharing'. However, posting a song on the Internet and making it available to a mass audience cannot be considered 'sharing' because of the potential magnitude of the exchange. We must consider the impact on the artist. Making one copy of a song from a purchased CD and sharing that copy with another individual is a limited exchange that will most likely not impact the artist's ability to earn revenue from his or her music. However, if that artist's music is posted on the Internet and available to a mass audience there is a significant possibility that the artist's CD sales will be reduced.

While any artist must accept that when he makes his work public he must relinquish some degree of control, copyright law exists to protect that artist's essential right to profit from his or her own work. Although those who exchange music for free over the Internet do not themselves profit from the transaction they do deprive musicians of the right to control the distribution of their own work. Purchasing a CD does not grant an individual the power to distribute an artist's work across a mass medium. Nor does the availability of music on the Internet make it acceptable to download songs without compensating the artist. As the free file sharing websites do not offer any means of compensating the artists, those who download songs are violating the artists' copyright and essentially stealing their work.

Some proponents of file sharing have argued that the only parties that suffer from free music downloads are the record companies. Even if this is the case, the infringement on the copyright of the artist by free file sharing is nonetheless detrimental to musicians. Musicians rely on record companies to produce and distribute their work. If the arrangement between the musicians and the record companies is somehow unfair to the artists, as some advocates of file sharing have suggested, the erosion of the artists' copyright protection through illegal distribution of their work is not the solution. Copyright protection is the musician's most important safeguard, and any infringement of that right, including free music downloads, must be regarded as stealing if we believe in artists' ultimate ownership of their creative works.

Word count: 545

2. Professional athletes should be barred from participating in the Olympics. Do you agree?

In recent years, certain Olympic events have been opened to professional athletes. Some people have renounced this change to one of the Olympics' most fundamental rules. Requiring athletes to maintain amateur status has been viewed as a means of keeping the international event free from commercial corruption. However, those who would cling to the amateur status rule fail to acknowledge how the world of sport has changed since the founding of the modern games. By limiting the Olympics to amateurs, the finest athletes in certain sports would never have the chance to compete for their countries or, alternatively, some of the world's most compelling events would be excluded from the games. The Olympics Committee was wise to bend an antiquated to rule in order to ensure that the games continue to be a relevant arena in the highly competitive world of modern sports.

The modern Olympics were conceived at a time when the majority of athletes, particularly in the events featured in the games, were amateurs. However, in the more than one hundred years since the founding of the modern games, the sporting world has changed dramatically. Today, many sports have shifted from amateur pursuits akin to serious hobbies to major industries. In order to pursue certain sports and compete against the best in the field athletes must turn professional. For these sports, we cannot expect major talents to forgo the opportunity to compete professionally, possibly during their athletic prime, in order to wait up to four years for the chance to participate in the Olympics. To restrict certain events to amateurs would mean making the level of play vastly inferior, and making the Olympics an irrelevant event in that particular sport.

Some argue that those sports that are essentially professional—various team sports and other "big money" individual events—should simply be eliminated from the Olympics. This is another example of the antiquated thinking that could make the Olympics obsolete. The purpose of the Olympics is to provide an arena in which international goodwill can be fostered through sports competitions. If the Olympics Committee is to accomplish its mission, it must draw a wide audience, and the best way to keep the public watching is to include sports that interest people—and for most people this means professional sports. Of course, some amateur sports—track and field or gymnastics, for example—draw a wide audience. However, if 'professional' sports are banned and the balance of the competition is made up of obscure sports, the Olympics will lose an opportunity to reach a wide audience.

Finally, although there is a romantic attachment to the ideal of the amateur athlete, in many ways shackling athletes to their amateur status limits the games to those who can afford to dedicate their personal finances to training at the Olympic level. The cost of pursuing a sport has changed significantly since the founding of the Olympics. Amateur athletes are so in name only; they are not pursuing their sport as a hobby but are completely dedicated to their event, practicing fulltime at great expense—something that only the financially well off can do. If, on the other hand, Olympic athletes were permitted to also compete professionally, talented athletes of lesser means might have an opportunity to participate in the Olympics. As professionals, athletes from all backgrounds have access to the best training and equipment, and the financial compensation they receive allows them to dedicate themselves full time to their sport. By opening the games to professional competitors, the Olympics have paradoxically become more egalitarian and more relevant than a strictly amateur event.

Word count: 597

3. Extraordinary measures are justified in order to protect endangered species from extinction. How do you respond to this statement?

Only a tiny fraction of the species that once walked the earth exist today. Evolution itself, the process by which all the species we know today came into being, depends on the extinction of 'failed' species. So why do we lament, and even take extreme measures to prevent, the extinction of one particular species? Often the species in question is one that is seen to have a unique value: an animal or plant of especial beauty or grace whose loss would be keenly felt. However, if we approach the issue from a purely environmental standpoint, that is if we leave human economic and social concerns out of the equation, we must question the sense of taking extreme measures to save one particular species. Pouring money into schemes to save one endangered species—often for sentimental reasons—is not the best use of the limited funds available to address serious environmental concerns.

The viability of any species is intimately linked to the survival of its habitat. Most species today are failing not because of some inherent evolutionary weakness but due to the destruction of their habitats—well-adapted species are suddenly doomed when humans raze their forests or drain their wetlands. Given the importance of habitats to the survival of numerous species, we would be better served to spend our money preserving particularly species rich environments rather than one endangered species. The gain in terms of biodiversity we would achieve by preserving one acre of rainforest—some of which are so dense with animal and plant life we have not even begun to catalogue the species living there—would far outweigh the benefit of saving a lone species.

Although some campaigns to save 'valuable' species, such as the whales, have been very successful not only at preserving species from extinction but galvanizing the public's interest in the environment in general, we must be wary of these efforts. For the most part these campaigns aim to protect appealing creatures. Although people might readily rally to save such magnificent animals as whales or panthers, the efforts to preserve these animals do not necessarily make the most sense from a scientific point of view. There are vast numbers of species on Earth, particularly in the oceans, that have not even been catalogued let alone put on an endangered species list—their fate notwithstanding. And, the majority of species that face extinction are insects and other unappealing animals that are unlikely to generate an outpouring of support. However, their lack of 'cuteness' does not mean these species are any less valuable from an ecological standpoint than the endangered black panther.

All the plants and animals coexisting in a certain environment play an important role in preserving the health of that biosphere. To single out one particular, often appealing, species for special protection fails to recognize the interconnectedness of each environment. By funneling money into extreme measures to save one species we may miss an opportunity to save vast numbers of endangered species by protecting a marshland or rainforest from destruction. Our limited resources must be used where they will have the greatest environmental impact not in expensive efforts to pull one 'appealing' species from the brink of destruction.

Word count: 532

4. The public's fascination with celebrity culture is a dangerous social trend. How do you respond to this statement?

Most young people today are more likely to be able to recount the life story of Victoria Beckham than that of Margaret Thatcher. The media is flooded with celebrity 'news' and the public seems to have an insatiable appetite for gossip. While people have always followed the lives of actors, athletes, and other famous people, today's fascination with celebrity culture is completely out of proportion, so much so that it represents a serious threat to the national culture. The public interest in celebrities and their exploits draws attention away from serious news, debases the national intellect, and erodes public morality.

Media is a business that caters to the public. If people crave celebrity gossip, this is what the media will provide. As a result, the coverage of international events and domestic politics will necessarily diminish, and the public will become even less interested in serious journalism and ever more captivated by celebrity culture. This lack of interest in international affairs and domestic politics has a serious impact. Politicians respond to public pressure. If our public is more interested by happenings in Hollywood than in Whitehall, politicians will not be motivated to change or turn their attention to matters that desperately need political intervention.

The public interest in celebrity culture not only draws attention away from more serious matters, it erodes the people's ability to engage with complex issues. If people devote their spare time to reading gossip magazines and watching celebrity news programmes, they are, by default, not reading or viewing material that challenges them intellectually or informs them about their world. As a result, Britons are losing their command of basic historical and geographic information and are instead experts on the romantic histories of a handful of 'famous' people. Not only are people less informed, their intellects are dulled by a diet of reading material written at a juvenile level. People who are accustomed to articles devoid of complex sentences that can be read in a few minutes will lose their tolerance for longer and more nuanced fare.

Finally, we must consider the content of celebrity 'news' and its impact on the national culture. A quick survey of gossip magazines will reveal stories about infidelities, divorces, material excesses, and indulgences in drink and drugs. If our nation's young people aspire to emulate the lives of celebrities, we can hardly be surprised if binge drinking is on the rise and there seems to be a general decline in moral values. The national obsession with celebrity teaches young people to value appearance over substance and material wealth over intellectual and cultural achievement. While the celebrities themselves may not aspire to be role models or enjoy being emulated, the glut of gossip, which naturally focuses on salacious details, has an undeniably negative influence.

While for many people catching up on celebrity gossip is a harmless diversion, the encroachment of celebrity 'news' into our culture represents a dangerous trend. Of course, reports about celebrities are in and of themselves not necessarily harmful, if they are not one's sole source of information. The danger lies in the fact that celebrity news has replaced more serious reporting and more intellectually challenging material. A nation that knows more about a one-time pop star than a former national leader is in a precarious cultural position.

Word count: 548

5. Should the use of performance-enhancing substitutes such as steroids be tolerated in the world of professional athletics? How do you respond to this question?

Our society is fascinated by sporting events. Athletes are among the most beloved celebrities, and may in some cases be more widely admired than film stars or politicians. With this fame comes astonishing wealth. As a result, a desire to gain a competitive edge over their rivals has led some professional athletes to use muscle-building substances, such as anabolic steroids, or other performance-enhancing supplements. No doubt these substances can help one to become stronger, to run faster, or to build endurance. As the potential rewards involved become ever greater, the drive to win at any cost comes with another enormous pressure. However, the question posed is certainly relevant from an ethical standpoint: Should athletes succumb to the lure of such substances? What of the potential health risks involved? Should these substances be subject to the rule of the respective governing bodies, or should these choices be left to individuals, regardless of the risks?

The 'benefits' to those who surreptitiously abuse steroids and other performance-enhancing substances are clear: Huge, muscle-bound performers achieve startling results and break records in every category. Spectators are enthralled, and attendances at sporting events rise. Schoolboys and stockbrokers alike feel obsessive interest in the minutiae of statistics established by these superstars. Franchise owners are particularly thrilled with their receipts, and lavish tremendous salaries and bonuses upon players, year after year.

These riches and fame based on performance-enhancing substances are not without their costs, however. The abuse of steroids is extremely damaging to the health of the athletes who decide to take them. This seems paradoxical, given that athletes must be in tip-top physical shape. Short-term gains in strength and endurance will inevitably give way to compromised well-being. The dangers involved in systematic steroid abuse involve various psychiatric disorders, such as the notorious " 'roid rage", which becomes fairly common after even a brief cycle of injecting the drugs. Other potential problems include extensive liver damage, and susceptibility to tumors and cancer. In extreme cases, even death may ultimately occur from the complications of the long-term abuse of steroids.

Given the fact that these enhancers are illegal, and are in fact dangerous drugs, it seems reasonable that their abuse should be strictly monitored by the respective governing bodies involved in the oversight of athletic activities. The problems with steroids and athletics became so widespread in the United States that the federal government was recently obliged to investigate into their abuse.

The matter generated a lot of publicity, and a few public acts of contrition, but little else. The problem is unlikely to disappear unless it is addressed openly and with the proper understanding and concern. The abuse of performance-enhancing drugs should not be tolerated. Professional athletes violating established rules prohibiting the used of banned or illegal substances should be punished accordingly. It's true that elite athletes are extremely gifted individuals, and they should be rewarded accordingly. But it should also be remembered that they are also much like the rest of us normal fans, in that they simply seek enjoyment in their lives, and to shine at what they do best. Counselling should be mandatory for athletes who have abused illegal substances. Hopefully, this would lend perspective, and remind them why they began to play the games they love in the first place. Professional athletes can remain competitive and perform spectacular feats without compromising their health, their integrity, and their personal happiness for misguided, short-term goals like records, titles, and contracts. Their fans will forgive them if they can accomplish these feats without flexing a pair of 30-inch biceps.

Word count: 596

| PART FIVE |

Appendixes

Appendix A: **A Brief Logic Primer**

The LNAT is not a test of formal logic. However, many of the multiple-choice questions assume familiarity with basic logic concepts such as the use of analogy in an argument and drawing inferences based on evidence provided. In your essays, you are asked to take a stance on the given issue and support that position with reasoned, competent arguments.

A primer in the basic structure of arguments and common logical errors will give you an edge.

BASIC ARGUMENT STRUCTURE

In logic, an **argument** is not a quarrel or dispute. Rather, it is a persuasive appeal involving two or more statements, including a conclusion and at least one premise (evidence to support that conclusion).

A **conclusion** is the main claim of the argument. The conclusion of an argument may take the form of a declarative statement, but it may also be embedded in a proposal, recommendation, plan, or prediction. It is only a conclusion as part of an argument; without the premise(s) to support it, it is simply an assertion or claim **that lacks support. Each essay prompt is itself a conclusion.**

Evidence and Conclusions

The conclusion is not necessarily the last point presented. It could just as well appear in the guise of a topic sentence, at the beginning of a passage, or in the middle of the passage, after a sentence or two of background exposition.

Common indicators of the **conclusion** include:

- therefore
- so
- hence
- thus
- accordingly
- consequently
- it follows that
- this proves/shows/suggests
- we can infer that
- which implies that
- should
- must
- clearly
- may be inferred from

Common verbal indicators of **evidence** (or **premises**) include:

- because
- since
- in as much as
- given that
- for the following reasons
- in view of the fact that

But many other conclusion indicators could easily be inserted before the final sentence:

> [Premise] Experts agree that to an overwhelming extent, perceived job prospects determine undergraduates' choice of field of study. [Premise] Currently, the most popular major at Brandywine is computer technology, which must be due to the success of our recent graduates in finding good jobs. [Conclusion] This proves that/Therefore/Accordingly/It follows that/Clearly our recruitment efforts would be much more

successful if we drew attention to our eminent professors in the field of computer technology and publicized the successes of our recent graduates in landing high-paying jobs.

All **claims** have a truth value; they are either true or false.

In a valid **deductive** argument, the conclusion ***must*** be true if all of the evidence is true.

All members of the volleyball team are over 6 feet tall.

Andrea is a member of the volleyball team.

Therefore, Andrea is over 6 feet tall.

Because of this, it is easy to leave one piece out—it is implied by the other statements. If a piece of evidence is unstated, it is an **assumption** made by the writer. If a conclusion is unstated, it can be **inferred**.

All members of the volleyball team are over 6 feet tall. Andrea is a member of the volleyball team. (Inference: Andrea is over 6 feet tall.)

All members of the volleyball team are over 6 feet tall, so Andrea must be over 6 feet tall. (Assumption: Andrea is a member of the team.)

In some cases, one or more of the premises will be false, so even if the conclusion is true, the argument will be unsound because it is based on one or more false premises.

On the other hand, it is important to bear in mind that even though an argument is defective, the conclusion may still be true; it is simply the argument that is invalid. Similarly, the fact that a conclusion is clearly true does not mean that the argument is strong or cogent because the premises may be problematic.

Logical Errors (Fallacies)

You will ***not be tested*** on the names of any logical errors, but being aware of the types of errors possible can build your confidence for the multiple-choice questions and will help you avoid building a weak argument in your essay. Questions asking you to choose an answer that strengthens or weakens argument often focus on inherent flaws in the writer's argument

Common sense alone is usually enough to identify these faults. Here is a brief review of the most common. (Answers to practice sets are at the end of the section.)

False Dilemma: The argument is based on a false dichotomy, reducing the audience's apparent options to one of two extremes. These are very common. For example:

1. The key to success is not competition but cooperation.
2. The goal of an educational system must be to instill values, not to provide vocational training.

Competition and cooperation are not mutually exclusive and there are many other possible keys to success. Educational systems have many goals, and instilling values and providing job training are both important. A good response to an argument that sets up such a false dichotomy might discuss some of the other goals and how to balance those with instilling values and job training. If you set up a dichotomy in your essay, be sure to provide your reasoning for it.

Practice 1

Prove that each of the following dilemmas is false by listing alternatives in the space provided.

1. The key to success is not competition but cooperation.

____

____

2. The goal of an educational system must be to instill values, not to provide vocational training.

____

____

3. Government should provide social services instead of wasting money on the arts.

____

____

4. If you're not going to work hard at your job, you should quit.

5. The challenger is so unskilled in chess that the champion will either lose the game and be humiliated or win and feel really guilty.

Overstated Generalization: Often such propositions make a broad statement about a specific group or institution:

> Professional athletes have a serious responsibility as role models.
>
> Government cannot support the arts without undermining them.
>
> It is not the place of schools to provide health education.

Other signs of the overstated generalization are superlatives ("the most important"), and extreme adverbs (never, always, rarely, only, everything, nothing, impossible or extremely):

> The chief lesson of history is that we have nothing to learn from it.
>
> Progress arises only out of disagreement and discontent.

In both form and content, these are frequently aphoristic: like proverbs, they are rhetorically balanced, morally instructive and somewhat paradoxical.

> Success is easy to achieve but difficult to enjoy.

Some arguments may even present false dilemmas embedded within overstated generalizations:

> An individual's attitudes are primarily determined by his or her character rather than by the particular situation in which they are evoked.

Statements like this often sound reasonable. Like false dilemmas, they don't consider alternatives. Overstated generalizations state one point of view, so think about alternatives in response to them.

Practice 2

Prove that the generalization is overstated by listing exceptions in the space provided.

1. Government should never seek to restrict the rights of individuals.

____

____

2. In business, the most important secret to success is originality.

____

____

3. In leadership, no skill is so rare and yet so vital as the ability to make decisions.

____

____

4. Any person who thinks schoolteachers have an easy job wouldn't last a day in most state schools.

____

____

5. The main goal of research should be practical technology that makes life more enjoyable for people in general.

____

____

6. In today's society, everyone thinks that style is more important than substance.

___

___

Appeal to Authority: It is frequently legitimate to invoke the views of authorities who have pertinent expertise and credibility. The argument will be less strong if it cites experts without establishing their credentials or if there is substantial disagreement among experts on the point in question. An argument based on anonymous authority is extremely weak, since the expertise of the authority cannot be verified. For example:

> Experts agree that to an overwhelming extent…

Who are these experts? The evidence attributed to anonymous experts may seem unobjectionable, but the appeal to authority is itself a weakness in the argument.

Inductive Fallacies: Deductive arguments are those in which the conclusion drawn ***must*** be true based on the evidence offered (assuming the evidence is true). **Inductive** arguments are those in which the conclusion drawn only ***might*** be true based on the evidence that is presented. Inductive reasoning frequently involves drawing inferences about a population as a whole based on information about a sample.

Inductive fallacies arise from inappropriate reliance on a sample. That is, the conclusion is drawn from a sample that is too small (hasty generalization), unrepresentative of the target population (unrepresentative sample), or not analogous to the target population (false analogy).

Practice 3

Identify the conclusion and evidence in this paragraph written by an American. Is the conclusion valid? Is it true?

> The following appeared in a memo from a member of the school board in the town of Delos. "For the past five years, Mr. Evan Brockhoff has been the head football coach at Central High School. During that time the varsity football team from Central High has won three state championships. In addition, the quality of the gymnasium and the athletic equipment at Central High has improved significantly over the past five years. Because of the outstanding achievements of Central High, the Delos school board should hire Mr. Brockoff as the general director in charge of athletic programs for the entire Delos school system."

Conclusion:

____

____

Evidence:

____

____

____

____

____

____

____

____

____

____

Hasty Generalization: When the size of the sample is too small to serve as a basis for the conclusion, we make hasty generalizations. Eat at a restaurant once, for example, and say the food is lousy. Hasty generalizations are apt to look like the following:

> Surveillance cameras installed in two of the town's fifteen municipal car parks show that the car parks are overcrowded, particularly 8:30 to 10:00, 11:30 to 1:00, and 4:00 to 5:30. Overcrowded car parks during these periods create hazards to drivers and pedestrians and increase congestion in nearby streets. Therefore, to alleviate congestion and improve safety, the town needs to build a new, multi-level municipal parking garage.

Common sense should tell you that two out of fifteen is not a large enough sample to come to the conclusion about all the car parks. These two car parks may be busier than the other thirteen—we don't know.

Unrepresentative Sample: An unrepresentative sample is one that differs in significant ways from the population as a whole. For example, if a study of sleep disorders is conducted on teenagers, but the results are projected on the entire population, including children and the elderly, the argument is invalid because the conclusions is based on an unrepresentative sample. Teenagers are a specific group within the population with specific characteristics that are not shared by other segments of the population. Likewise, the two car parks in the hasty generalization sample stimulus might not be representative of the car parks as a group.

Practice 4

In what way is the sample in this stimulus unrepresentative of the population about which the claim is made?

> Typically, as people age, the fatty deposits in their blood vessels (atherosclerosis) increase in size and number, making people more vulnerable to blood clots and blockages. A recent study concludes an effective way to reduce the risk of blockages in later life is to take aspirin daily. The four-year study followed a group of Belgian women in their eighties who were residents of assisted care facilities. The women were given daily dosages of aspirin. In addition, the women participated in an aquatic aerobics programme. After three years, these women showed a much lower rate of atherosclerosis than is average for their age.

Ways the sample is unrepresentative:

___

___

___

___

___

___

___

___

___

False Analogy: In making an analogy, one first establishes that two entities or situations are similar; then one implies that since the first term of comparison has a certain property, that property must also occur in the second term. A false analogy (comparing apples to oranges) occurs when the two terms compared differ in such a way as to invalidate the inferred commonality. For example:

> Our shopping centre franchise has 30% less seating than our city centre franchise, yet it produces nearly twice the daily revenue. The lack of seating often creates a crowded condition in the shop. This gives passers-by the impression that our products are highly desirable. If we want to increase in our city centre franchise, we should cut back on seating.

There are many problems with the logic in this argument, but a fundamental flaw is that the two franchises are not directly comparable because of their locations. Shopping centre traffic is likely to be heavier and steadier than a typical city centre location.

Practice 5

Identify the analogy and explain its weakness in this paragraph written by an American.

> When Stuckley's Family Buffet first opened, it was the largest, most heavily attended restaurant in town. It is still the largest restaurant, but it is no longer heavily used. A tally of table receipts last month revealed the restaurant's drop in popularity: the receipts showed an average of only 50 parties of diners per day. In contrast, tiny Javamunch Cafe in the heart of the business district is visited by more than 150 people on a typical weekday. An obvious difference is that Javamunch Café, unlike Stuckley's Buffet, provides full table service instead of buffet-style dining. Thus, if Stuckley's is ever to be as popular as Javamunch, the management will obviously need to provide full table service, thereby providing what customers want.

Analogy: ____

____

____

____

Weaknesses: ____

____

____

____

Post Hoc, Ergo Propter Hoc: The easiest causal error to identify is probably ***post hoc, ergo propter hoc*** ("after this, therefore because of this"). The fallacious assumption is that because X came before Y, it caused Y; here are three other important possibilities:

- X and Y might have independent causes
- X and Y might have the same cause
- X might have been only one of several causes.

Here's an example:

> Our shopping centre franchise put a new coat of paint on the walls, purchased potted plants, and put fresh flowers on the tables to coincide with the launch of our new value menu. In the first week of the new menu, its sales were 20% higher than all other franchises, and on many customer satisfaction surveys, clients specifically mentioned the new décor. To increase business at our other franchises, we should similarly upgrade the décor.

Of course, the improved décor came before the launch of the new menu, but is it likely the décor alone is responsible for the significantly higher percentage of sales? It certainly may be a factor, but there are too many other possible factors, including the knowns—the new value menu and the high-traffic location—and possible unknowns, such as advertising.

Practice 6

Identify the weakness in the causal argument embedded in this stimulus.

> The following appeared in a newspaper article published in the country of Saludia: "Ten years ago, one half of all citizens in Saludia met the standards for healthy height-to-weight ratios as then defined by the ministry of health and fitness. Today, the ministry says that only one quarter of all citizens meet the standards and suggests that the increasing prevalence of office

> jobs may be the reason. But since healthy height-to-weight levels are highest in regions of Saludia where levels of office employment are also highest, it is clear that working in offices has not made citizens less physically fit. Instead, as shown by this year's unusually low expenditures on fitness-related products and services, the recent decline in the economy is most likely the cause, and healthy weight levels will improve when the economy does."

Weaknesses: ____

____

____

____

Genuine but Insignificant Cause: Finally, there's the causal fallacy of putting too much weight on a real but insignificant cause. The argument neglects other pertinent and much more significant causes. Again, the shopping centre franchise situation (see "Post Hoc...") provides a good example. Sure, the new décor may have helped, but it is a less significant factor than the new value menu. Other more significant causes could include advertising and the business's location.

Suppressed Information: A valid argument must consider all relevant information. In many cases, a precedent or supposedly analogous case is introduced as evidence, but we cannot evaluate its relevance without pertinent data. The trick is to determine if essential information is missing or whether conclusions were drawn based on only part of the story.

The surveillance camera stimulus (see "Hasty Generalization") is a good example. We cannot legitimately accept or reject the conclusion without knowing how representative the two car parks are. We also need more information on the impact such a project would have on the community as well as how such a project would be funded.

Slippery Slope: The slippery slope claims that if X happens, then Y will definitely follow. But when there is no logical causal relationship—no reason why X necessarily leads to Y—you have slippery slope reasoning as in the following American-written example:

> Many companies have "casual Fridays" when employees have the opportunity to "dress down" and come to work in polos and slacks rather than suits and ties. But casual dress leads to a casual work ethic. People feel more professional when they are

> dressed professionally; thus they will feel less professional when they dress casually. In addition, one day of casual attire will affect professionalism throughout the week, and employees will attempt to wear more casual attire Monday until Thursday as well. Therefore, if we implement casual Fridays, we can expect to have a less productive and less professional workforce.

There are two slippery slopes in this argument: that casual Fridays will reduce professionalism throughout the week and that casual Fridays will result in a "less productive and less professional workforce." There may indeed be a relationship between attire and professionalism, but not necessarily of the sort predicted here. In fact, casual clothes might help people feel more relaxed and comfortable at work, which may in turn boost productivity (not to mention employee satisfaction).

PRACTICE ANSWERS AND EXPLANATIONS

Practice 1

1. Competition and cooperation are not mutually exclusive: think of team sports or corporate business ventures.

2. Educational systems have many goals; instilling values and providing job training are both important. Other goals include recreation, fitness training, and public service.

3. Government spending is more complicated than a choice between the arts and social services: a way can be found to afford both if they are both high priorities. Or, what about arts institutions such as museums, artists' colonies and grant programmes that provide social services (employment, daycare, support) and advance the arts at the same time?

4. It might show good work ethics to resign from a job that you're not enthusiastic about, but it is a false dilemma. Other alternatives include staying at your job but not working hard, or working hard and then leaving anyway.

5. Or maybe the chess champion will win and feel great anyway, or he or she will lose and be impressed, pleased or relieved.

Practice 2

1. Any of the many cases where the rights of individuals come into conflict with each other is a good exception to this generalization. For example, a restaurant owner's right to try and make a profit doesn't supersede the customer's right to healthy food: that's why we have health regulations.

2. There are many factors that contribute to commercial success: efficiency and quality are obviously important. Originality may be useful, but imitation can certainly be profitable.

3. There are many "vital" qualities for a leader. The ability to get other people to follow must be just as important as the ability to make decisions.

4. This generalization says that the only way to understand the difficulties that face state school teachers is to be one. That's not necessarily true: the difficulties can be understood by observation or study, or a person could be a teacher and still not think that it was difficult.

5. The generalization here lies in connecting "practical research" (whatever that is) with enjoyable life. A lot of technologies that make life more enjoyable—for example the graphite materials used in different kinds of sporting equipment—come from general or abstract research.

6. This statement contains a false dilemma (style and substance are not mutually exclusive), but it also contains an overstated generalization in the assertion that "everyone thinks" style is more important. Any example of a person or group that values substance over style refutes this generalization.

Practice 3

Conclusion: Brockhoff should become the athletic director of the district.

Premises:

- Mr. Brockhoff began as the head coach five years ago.
- In the last five years, the team has won three championships.
- In the last five years, the quality of athletic facilities has improved.

The conclusion here is invalid. The premises show that Mr. Brockhoff's tenure coincides with an improvement in the athletics programmes of the school, so you can infer a relationship. But it might just be a coincidence, or there may be a confusion between causes and effects here. For example, an improvement in the athletic equipment may have caused the championships without any contribution from the coach. Furthermore, there's no evidence to suggest that Mr. Brockhoff's ability as a football coach necessarily makes him a good general director. It's impossible to know whether the conclusion is true or not, but it isn't necessarily false either.

Practice 4

In this stimulus, the conclusion implicitly bears on all people of all ages. Yet the study group is extremely limited. Any of the distinguishing characteristics of the sample group (that the subjects were women, that they were Belgian, that they were over eighty years old, that they lived in assisted care, and that they exercised) could introduce factors that do not apply to the population as a whole.

Practice 5

In this instance, the differences in size and location between the two restaurants invalidate any inference you could make about the impact of table service on their relative popularity.

Practice 6

In this example, the drop in physical fitness is attributed to the economic recession on the grounds that expenditures on fitness-related products and services have dropped recently. Common sense should tell us that, at the national level, physical fitness is not determined by the amount spent on fitness products and services. In the best of times, the proportion of Saludians who even try to stay fit through such devices would probably not be enough to affect 25% of the population, and of those who tried even fewer would have seen significant results. It is much more likely that the correlation is coincidental than causal.

Appendix B: **The Writing Process**

You probably know by now that a good written product comes from a good writing process. Whether you tend to brainstorm and organize in your head or put everything down on paper, whether you like to write one draft or ten, your writing will come out stronger when you start with a plan, write out your ideas and then revise and **edit your work.**

In most real-life writing situations, you have plenty of time to work through each of these writing stages. But for the LNAT essay you have only 40 minutes, so having a reliable, efficient process is even more important.

So here's a review of the writing process as it specifically applies to writing a timed essay for the LNAT.

TIMING

This first three steps in Kaplan's method (1. Select a topic and decide your position, 2. Make a rough outline, and 3. Develop detail in your outline) are also perhaps the most essential for a timed essay. Planning and outlining should take about 1/4 of your test time (save half for the actual writing, and another 1/4 for revising and editing). So for a 40-minute essay, spend about 10 minutes planning before you begin to write your essay.

SELECTING YOUR POSITION

Before brainstorming, before outlining, before you do anything else, make sure you understand the writing task. Exactly what is it that you are being asked to do? What will the readers be looking for?

The prompt is intended to provoke, by presenting a strong point of view on an issue and asking you to take a stance. Sometimes it will seem to you that the question is obvious, that only one particular point of view is possible. This is a mistake—there are definitely at least two sides to each issue offered. You must choose a side, but the best essays also analyze your choice and show how it compares to other alternatives.

For example, let's look at the following :

> A university education should be available to only the most talented students.

Before you take a side, consider all of the possible positions. First the obvious ones—that university education should be available to everyone and that it should only be available to the most talented students. Clearly there are other alternatives. For example, some of our institutions are highly selective, while others are open to anyone. Yet even the most selective universities espouse a policy of inclusiveness, with admissions policies that take into account a variety of non-academic factors. And even those with the most lenient admissions policies still have academic standards that effectively prevent the least talented students from obtaining a degree. Whatever position you choose, it's best to both take a position and show that you have considered a whole range of possibilities.

Brainstorm Ideas

Now that your task is clear, it's time to start brainstorming ideas. Do you know what position you want to take or do you need to think about it? Think it through on paper.

Brainstorming Techniques.

Brainstorming simply refers to the technique of focusing on a particular problem or issue to come up with ideas. For a timed essay, try listing or freewriting. Write down whatever comes to your mind about the topic. Remember that in a brainstorm, *anything goes*. Don't discount any ideas yet—you're still in the planning stage, and an idea that doesn't seem relevant now can lead you to another that may form the crux of your argument. Forget about grammar, sentence structure, or anything else that might hinder your thoughts. Just get your ideas down. If you don't know where to start, try writing the main issue or question and answering it.

If you don't know which position you will take, first brainstorm to determine your thesis. If you know as soon as you read the stimulus what position you would like to argue, then jump right into the second step: brainstorming support for your argument. It can be helpful to brainstorm ideas for opposing points of view so you can address counterarguments in your essay.

Below are examples of brainstorming for an essay in response to the following statement:

> A university education should be available to only the most talented students.

Listing means just that—list whatever ideas come to mind. In the sample list below, the author starts with a series of questions that leads to more concrete ideas to be used as the basis of the essay.

Is education a right or privilege? BOTH

Right: To what level?

Why cut off at secondary school? (Cost prohibitive?)

Privilege: Must be earned—but how?

Who earns that privilege?

Who decides who's earned it?

What kind of talent? Not just academic, also dedication

Problem: how to define talent

*Democracy vs. meritocracy

More educated populace = good for EVERYONE

Less ignorance (thus more tolerance, better health care, etc.)

More skilled work force

Less poverty

More active in community and politics

Another approach, freewriting, is a free narrative response to develop ideas unencumbered by the conventions of essay writing (no worries about grammar, paragraphing, cohesion, etc.). For example, consider the following statement:

> Perceived job prospects should determine a university student's choice of field of study.

Here's a freewriting approach:

> OK, perceived job prospects are important but my initial reaction is they put too much weight on this. Most people I know didn't choose their degree because of potential jobs but because they like the field, or if they did choose because of a specific job its because they think they'll like that career, of course if there's a high demand for a particular career that does make it more appealing, but for example I'd never switch from biology to computer technology simply because there's a lot of highpaying jobs waiting for me upon graduation. I think comp tech is so popular because kids like computers, not <u>just</u> because those undergrads want good jobs. Another prob: doubt that it's the most popular field of study because of the success of recent grads. That's always a boost, because it's evidents of a good programme. But is that what recruiting should focus on? Yes, eminent profs and grad success rates are important but recruitment should also focus on solidity of programme. And what about the other programmes at B? What % of students are comp tech students and how that fits into the overall mission/departmts/programmes at the school.

BUILDING YOUR OUTLINE

Once you've brainstormed ideas, it's time to put them—quickly—into a logical order. Again, it might be tempting to just jump in and write, but resist that temptation. A good outline will make the actual writing of your essay much easier and help minimize revisions.

The goal of an outline is twofold:

(1) to put the ideas you brainstormed into a logical order and

(2) to help ensure that you have enough support for each assertion you make.

By laying everything out before you write, you can see if you have any gaps in support or logic in your argument. If so, you can fix those problems before it's too late. You can also map out a logical sequence of ideas so that your argument or analysis flows smoothly from one paragraph to another.

A Well-Organized Outline = A Well-Organized Essay

You may tend to resist writing outlines for your normal writing tasks, but when writing under time pressure it's too important a step to ignore. Readers are looking for logical organization at every level of the essay, from the broad structure down to the individual sentence.

At the broadest level, the essay must have a beginning, a middle, and an end. The introductory paragraph must engage the stimulus, state the thesis, and lay out the plan for the body of the essay. The body of the essay must present two to four well-developed points in support of the claim staked out in the introduction. The conclusion should summarize the essay as a whole.

Too often, though, this three-part structure becomes something of a "list sandwich": the introduction and conclusion are just there to hold an undifferentiated list of points. As a result, the reader has no idea where the argument is going. While it is not necessary to declare explicitly the rationale behind your organization, you should definitely lay out your points in a clear trajectory. That is, your supporting ideas must be arranged in some logical sequence, even if there is no logical necessity to that sequence. Here are some of the possibilities:

- You might deploy your arguments in order of importance, or in order of accessibility or complexity (most obvious to most subtle, least complicated to most intricate).

Or you can let the subject matter be your guide and arrange your points by

- chronology
- cause and effect
- comparison and contrast
- analysis or classification
- problem-solution
- scale (scale can be perceived along many gradients. Here are just a few examples:
  - local, regional, national, global
  - individual, family, neighborhood, community, society
  - microscopic, organic, systemic
  - employee, department, division, corporation

Once you've determined your overall organizing principle, outline your major supporting points and the specific evidence and examples you can use to support each of those main points. Here's an example:

1. Intro: University education is a right, not just a privilege. It should be available to every citizen, and those with talent should be offered extra opportunities.
2. Why it's a right: democracy not meritocracy
    a. Country founded on democratic principle, all created equal, equal opportunity
        i. Principle used throughout primary and secondary schooling
        ii. Used in work force, government, law enforcement
        iii. Why not higher ed?
        iv. Counterargument: secondary school should be enough to satisfy equality for all principle. Rebuttal: lack of university education limits a whole segment of population, keeps them at lower wages, lower socio-economic status (transition to next para)
3. Why meritocracy is a problem
    a. Few in control of many (who decides who can go to university?)
    b. How do you define "talented"?
    c. Ripe for corruption
4. Benefits of equal opportunity
    a. Less ignorance (thus more tolerance, better health care, less drugs/violence, etc.)
    b. More skilled workforce
    c. Less poverty
    d. More involvement in community and politics
5. Conclusion (restate thesis)

A Well-Developed Outline = A Well-Developed Essay

Your outline can show you which paragraphs need more support. Do you have enough ideas and information to cover each topic thoroughly? Do you cover everything you need to cover, including counterarguments? For example, in the sample outline, the author does not address counterarguments in paragraphs 3 and 4, and paragraph 3 in general could use more development or support.

WRITING YOUR ESSAY

Now that you have a detailed outline, the actual writing of your essay should go rather smoothly, since you know what you want to say and the order in which you want to say it.

Introductions: Get Off to a Strong Start

In regular academic writing, your essay introductions typically have two main goals: (1) to grab the reader's attention and (2) to clearly state your thesis. In your LNAT essay, however, your focus should emphatically be on the latter. Right from the start, readers need to know the main idea of your essay.

What about grabbing the reader's attention with a catchy introduction? A real attention-grabber might impress a reader. Our advice: if you can immediately think of a catchy introduction, then by all means, use it. However, you don't have time to waste thinking of a good attention-grabber, so if it doesn't come to you right away, use a standard introduction.

Template for a Standard Introduction

1. Begin by briefly paraphrasing the issue or summarizing the argument.
2. State your thesis.
3. Outline the main points to be covered in your essay (in the order in which you will cover them).

Example:

> A university education should be available to only the most talented students.

I emphatically disagree. Limiting access to higher education to a small percentage of our population undermines our democracy and hurts our society on many levels—socially, economically, and even morally. It also creates a host of problems in selecting those who are "most talented". Academic talent does deserve to be rewarded—but not at the expense of everyone else.

Here's slightly less standard beginning:

> Why should only the most talented students be allowed the chance to attend university? This opportunity should be available to all citizens, not just the academic elite. Limiting access to higher education to a small percentage of our population undermines our democracy and hurts our society on many levels—socially, economically and even morally. It also creates a host of problems in selecting those who are "most talented". Academic talent does deserve to be rewarded—but not at the expense of everyone else.

Write a Strong Thesis Statement

First, here's what a thesis statement is ***not***:

- A thesis statement is not a question: *"Is higher education a right or a privilege?"*
- A thesis statement is not a paraphrase of the stimulus: *"Some argue that higher education is a right; others that it is a privilege."*
- A thesis statement is not a general statement about the topic: *"There is much debate about whether higher education is a right or a privilege."*

Now here's what a thesis statement *is*:

A sentence that makes an assertion about the topic and clearly expresses the main idea of the essay:

> Access to higher education is a right, not a privilege.

For your essay, a good thesis statement clearly states your position on the issue (what you think and why you think it).

Write Strong Paragraphs

A paragraph is a group of sentences about a single idea. Make sure each paragraph has a clear topic sentence stating that main idea. In your regular writing you may be more subtle, but for the LNAT—given your readers (a tired reader who's read too many of these essays already)—you want to be as transparent as possible.

Develop Ideas

There's no magic number for how many sentences should be in a paragraph, because this depends upon the length of sentences and the purpose of the paragraph. For example, there are times when a short, one-sentence paragraph is rhetorically effective; likewise, there are times when a seven or eight sentence paragraph is appropriate. But the LNAT is not the place for either.

To play it safe on the exam, aim for four or five sentence paragraphs throughout your essay. In general, that's about what it takes, given average sentence lengths, to fully develop an idea: one topic sentence, two or three sentences with specific examples or evidence, and perhaps a sentence or two acknowledging and refuting counterarguments or providing a transition into the next paragraph.

The only exception to this guideline for paragraph length might be the conclusion, which is likely to be shorter than other paragraphs because there isn't a new idea to develop, but rather a position to restate.

Organize Ideas

You've already decided upon your overall principle of organization in your outline. Readers will be looking for organization at paragraph level as well as sentence level.

1. ***Paragraph unity.*** Does each paragraph deal with a single coherent idea? Do any extraneous ideas creep in to distract the reader's attention?
2. ***Topic sentences.*** Does each paragraph have one main idea clearly stated in a topic sentence? We all know that the topic sentence can occur anywhere in the paragraph. Perfectly good paragraphs may even lack a topic sentence. But on the exam, play it safe. If at all possible, deploy a fully-developed topic sentence at the opening of each paragraph.
3. ***Transitional phrases***. Are there smooth and effective transitions between and within paragraphs? Your entire essay should be stitched together with transitional phrases. From the second paragraph to the conclusion, each topic sentence should begin with a conspicuous signpost marking the trajectory of your argument: ***the first problem, first of all, second, furthermore, one additional factor, in conclusion,*** etc. Within each paragraph, use signals that will draw the reader's attention to what you are doing: ***such as, for example, an alternative explanation, on the one hand/on the other, by contrast, however, nonetheless, consequently, therefore*** and so on.

Vary Sentence Structure: Whatever you actually say in your essay, ***how*** you say it can have a significant impact on your effectiveness. Your essay can be correct, concise, appropriate—yet still be dull and dry and at risk boring the reader.

Readers appreciate a variety of sentence forms. What that means, specifically, is that you'll want to use a combination of simple, compound, complex, and compound-complex sentences.

If you find that you tend to write using one type of sentence, practice rewriting your sentences in other structures to ensure that you use a variety on test day. Here are some examples:

Simple (one main clause):

> Any entrepreneur seeking a new business location should seriously consider Nashville, Tennessee.

Compound (two or more main clauses):

> Entrepreneurs often need to select a new business location, and they should seriously consider Nashville, Tennessee.

Complex (one main clause, one subordinate clause):

> If any entrepreneurs are looking for a new business location, they should seriously consider Nashville, Tennessee.

Compound-complex (two or more main clauses, plus at least one subordinate clause):

> Entrepreneurs often need to select a new business location, and when they do, they should seriously consider Nashville, Tennessee.

In addition to using a variety of these basic sentence forms, you can enliven your sentences by varying the order in which you use phrases and clauses within a sentence:

> X is unlike Y because of Z.
>
> Because of Z, X is unlike Y.
>
> However, X is unlike Y because of Z.
>
> X, however, is unlike Y because of Z.
>
> However, because of Z, X is unlike Y.

Practice 1

Fill in the table below. Each sentence is provided in either simple, compound, complex, or compound-complex form. Rewrite each given example in the three other forms. No answers are provided, since there aren't wrong or right variants. Just practise writing in sentence structures that you don't use often enough, so that they come more naturally to you on test day. For more practice, rewrite sentences you find in your reading.

Simple : Sometimes the fresh perspective of a non-expert can be valuable in the consideration of a subject.

Compound: ______________________________

____

Complex: ______________________________

____

Compound-Complex: ______________________________

____

Simple: ______________________________

____

Compound: The feeling of having fulfilled a personal goal is important, but the tangible rewards of society are at least as important.

Complex: ______________________________

____

Compound-Complex: ______________________________

____

Simple: ____

____

Compound: ____

____

Complex : Even though Company B is more expensive, the important question is whether the combined cost of pest-control and savings in product damage are greater with Company B.

Compound-Complex: ____

____

Simple: ____

____

Compound: ____

____

Complex: ____

____

Compound-Complex: Different academic communities have different traditions, and while these differences may be significant, it is an oversimplification to say that there can be no meaningful interaction between them.

Vary Sentence Length: A short sentence (four to eight words) can effectively emphasize a simple point; a long sentence (30–45 words) might be necessary to present a relatively complicated idea. Varying sentence length also creates a more pleasing rhythm for your readers—too many short sentences are likely to sound choppy.

> Entrepreneurs often need to select a new business location, and when they do, they should seriously consider Nashville, Tennessee. This southern city has a great deal to offer.

Vary Vocabulary: Repetition can be one of the most effective rhetorical devices when used deliberately, but it's the easiest way to bore the reader when used badly. One of the most important sentence-level strategies is to use synonyms instead if relying on a few key words throughout your essay.

> Repetitive: Business is not an occupation for the faint of heart. Every businessperson should be aware that nearly 50% of businesses fail in their first year, while 75% of businesses go under within three years. Our first order of business in this essay is to consider the question, "What are the causes of business failure?"

> Enriched: Business is not an occupation for the faint of heart. Every entrepreneur should be aware that nearly 50% of new ventures fail in their first year, while 75% go under within three years. Our first concern in this essay is to consider the question, "What are the causes of commercial failure?"

An effective way to avoid repetition, if this tends to be one of your weaknesses, is to make lists of terms pertinent to the various prompt topics. For example, here is a clustered list of nouns that might be useful when answering a question about higher education. If this tends to be one of your problems, jot down such a list before you start writing your essays.

- facilities, campus, library, laboratory, location, faculty-to-student ratio, sports
- recruitment, scholarship, financial aid, stipend, assistance, promotional material, catalogue, publication, publicity, public relations
- admissions, requirements, standards, entrance, application
- administration, administrator, dean, official, board of trustees, committee
- faculty, professor, advisor, candidate, academic, researcher, lecturer, teaching assistant, educator
- student, applicant, candidate, alumnus, registrant, undergraduate, graduate, scholar, researcher
- field, research, study, discipline, programme
- instruction, courses, curriculum, lecture, seminar, workshop, lab, syllabus, assigned

readings, assignments, homework

- grades, marks, scores, average, points
- test, competition, examination, quiz, final
- university, institution, higher education, academia, school
- goals, objectives, degree, graduation, commencement, employment, career, job, placement, opportunity

Practice 2

The following paragraph contains examples of overly repetitive word use. Correct the problems by rewriting the paragraph with appropriate synonyms in place of the repetitive words and phrases.

> Courses that focus on intellectual development are more important than courses that contribute to professional development. Courses focused on professional development assume that these courses will still be relevant to the future job market, while in fact the constant changes in the job market might make such courses obsolete. In contrast, courses that work toward intellectual development are courses that train a person for a variety of job market roles, so that even if the job market changes, the work done in the courses remains relevant. This is not to say that many courses cannot do both: preparing a person for the job market while also preparing her for a variety of different job market possibilities. But, while courses on professional development have their place in the realm of university courses, they should not be allowed to supersede courses that train the intellect for a changing job market.

Answers to this exercise will vary. In addition to merely replacing a word with a synonym, you may find that changing the sentence structure avoids the need for repetition.

Repetitive words and phrases in this paragraph: courses, development, job market

Synonyms for "courses": lessons, classes, curricula, programmes, learning, education

Synonyms for "development": improvement, training, education, advancement, enhancement

Synonyms for "job market": employment, professional setting, occupation, trade, the business world

Sample essay using synonyms:

> In designing a curriculum, it is more important to focus on intellectual improvement than on professional training. An educational programme that emphasizes the latter assumes that this education will still be relevant to a student's future occupation, when in fact constant changes in the job market might make such learning obsolete. In contrast, a course of study that works toward intellectual growth prepares a person for a variety of occupations, so that even if the demands of employers change, the curriculum remains relevant. This is not to say that many educational programmes cannot do both: preparing a person for employment in a specific field while also preparing her for a variety of possible vocations. But, while classes that provide professional training have their place in the university curriculum, they should not be allowed to supersede education that trains the intellect for a changing job market.

Write Your Conclusion

Think for a moment about the last movie you saw. What's the first scene that comes to mind? Chances are you best remember the beginning or the end of the film. For better or for worse, first and final impressions do count, and this is especially true in writing essays that will be read quickly as one of hundreds. Indeed, conclusions often have the power to make or break an essay. A weary human reader, for example, might be well satisfied throughout your essay only to be disappointed by a weak conclusion.

As we've said many times now, your best bet is to play it safe throughout your essay, and this includes the conclusion. You want your ending to have impact, but you don't have the time or the rhetorical freedom to perfect anything fancy with your conclusion (and the reader probably won't pick up on any sophisticated rhetorical techniques). Instead, stick to a standard conclusion that:

1. restates your main idea and
2. briefly summarizes your main support.

Your conclusion should ***not***:

- Repeat the thesis statement in exactly the same words. Your essay is too short for direct repetition. When you restate your main idea, make sure it's an effective paraphrase.
- Open a new topic. A good conclusion will provide a sense of closure so that readers feel as if the topic has been covered methodically and completely.

REVISING AND EDITING YOUR ESSAY

Typically writers are advised to revise first (addressing big-picture issues of organization and development and sentence-level issues such as structure and word choice) and then edit for purely mechanical improvements (like spelling, grammar, and punctuation). But your time on the LNAT is limited. If you used your planning and writing time effectively, you will only have about 10 minutes left to review your essay, so revise and edit simultaneously.

Big Picture Checklist

Your essay should:

- State ideas clearly. Do you have a thesis statement at the beginning of your essay? Do you have topic sentences in each paragraph?
- Develop ideas fully. Do you explain your ideas completely? Do you provide strong and specific support?
- Organize ideas logically. Do you have an effective organising principle for your essay? Within your paragraphs? Have you paragraphed effectively?
- Stay focused. Does your essay digress from your main idea? Is all of your support relevant?
- Signpost constantly. Do you use strong transitions within and between paragraphs?

Sentence-Level Checklist

On the sentence level:

- Are your sentences correct? Can you find and correct any errors in grammar or mechanics?
- Are your sentences clear? Are there any ambiguous or vague sentences?
- Are your sentences concise? Can you eliminate any unnecessary repetition or wordiness?

- Are your sentences precise? Have you used exact words and phrases as well as specific details?
- Are your sentences assertive? Do you state your points without hesitation?
- Are your sentences at the appropriate level of formality, tone and point of view throughout?
- Do you vary sentence structure and vocabulary?

Practice 3

Each of the following is a paragraph that might appear in an LNAT essay. Each paragraph includes numerous errors. Practise proofreading by locating and correcting them.

Excerpt 1

(1) The advise given to the company managers that hiring more additional workers will result in a larger number of houses being built was unwise. (2) Several pieces of extremely vital information are not taken into consideration in the reasoning that more workers means more houses built, a moments reasoning reveals that many factors other then merely the number of workers determines the answer to the question of how many houses will be built? (3) For example, if the construction company doesn't have enough construction equipment/tools to equip more worker's, then extra workers won't help irregardless. (4) If there aren't enough building sights available, a raw materials shortage, or sufficient infrastructure to support additional workers, then hiring more workers might well been just a waste of money. (5) The whole question of diminishing returns is not considered by this line of reasoning at all in increasing staff size.

Excerpt 2

(1) While the School Boards argument that eating breakfast is related to a reduction of absenteeism in the school breakfast programme may be convincing. (2) The conclusion that forcing more students to eat breakfast on the school programme will cause a decreasing drop in absences is unwarranted. (3) The statistic's show a correspondance that is far from clear enough to assume causation. (4) The attendance of students at the school-sponsored breakfast programme and at subsequent classes maybe both result from a third, unexamined cause that creates the observed affect. (5) For example, students who eat school breakfasts everyday might just happen to be the ones who go to bed early, and therefore are up in time for both the breakfast and for classes. (6) Or maybe the students with better attendance experience a different kind of parent supervision that contributes to both one's better diet and their improved attendance.

Excerpt 3

(1) In surveying their customers and found that they prefer games with lifelike graphics, the computer game company has correctly identified a cause for an increase in the popularity of particular game types. (2) From the evidence presented it seems okay to think that certain customers might maybe buy the

more lifelike games in preference to games with worse graphics. (3) However, the conclusion that game sales will rise as an end result of this action neglects to take into account the evidence. (4) That the more lifelike games require the latest new computer hardware. (5) The argument presents no evidence to show the fact that the target audience is undergoing a transition to this more advanced and more expensive type of computer platform. On the contrary common sense seems perhaps to suggest that, since the target audience tends to be young, that their earning power would not allow them to acquire the equipment necessary to accomodate the games in question, and thus it would not necessarily result in increased sales of those games. (7) If the company was to invest in developement of these games, they might waste money in the end.

Answers and Explanations to Practice 3

Excerpt 1

(1) ***Advice*** is the noun; advise is a verb.

More additional is an example of pleonasm (redundancy).

Advice is the singular subject of the sentence, so it takes the singular verb form, *contains*.

(2) ***Extremely*** *vital is redundant.*

This sentence is a run-on—two independent clauses joined by a comma with no conjunction. Fix it by either adding a conjunction or by making it into two sentences (or possibly by swapping the comma for a semicolon).

Moment's is possessive, so it takes an apostrophe.

Reasoning repeats the preceding clause, so replace it with another term such as *thought.*

The sentence compares the number of workers with the other factors, so the comparative *than* is required.

The final question is embedded, so it uses a full stop rather than a question mark.

(3) Omit the slash as a substitute for the conjunction ***or*** in essays.

Workers is a simple plural here, so no apostrophe is necessary.

The word is regardless rather than ***irregardless***.

(4) The sentence here refers to building locations (sites), not things seen (sights).

The middle term in this series violates parallelism in the original, creating confusion.

The future conditional subjunctive here takes the verb be rather than ***been***.

(5) The phrase ***in increasing staff size*** modifies the question of diminishing returns, so put the modifier next to the thing it modifies in order to avoid confusion.

Excerpt 2

(1) While the school board's argument that eating breakfast in the school breakfast programme is related to a reduction of absenteeism may be convincing. (2) The conclusion that forcing more students to eat breakfast on the school programme will cause a decrease in absences is unwarranted. (3) The statistics show a correspondence that is far from clear enough to assume causation. (4) The attendance of students at the school-sponsored breakfast programme and at subsequent classes might both result from a third, unexamined cause that creates the observed effect. (5) For example, students who eat school breakfasts every day might just happen to be the ones who go to bed early [no comma] and therefore are up in time for both the breakfast and for classes. (6) Or perhaps the students with better attendance experience a different kind of parent supervision that contributes to both their better diet and their improved attendance.

(1) ***School board*** is a common noun, so no capitals. If it were the name of a specific school board, for example the Shelby County School Board, then it would be capitalized.

In the school breakfast programme modifies ***eating breakfast***, so it should go closer to what it modifies in order to avoid confusion about what exactly is in the programme.

This sentence is a fragment because of the subordinate "while" at the beginning. One easy way to fix this problem is to join it to the next sentence by changing the full stop to a comma and eliminating the capital letter at the beginning of the next sentence.

(2) ***Decreasing drop*** is redundant.

(3) ***Statistics*** is a simple plural, not a possessive, so no apostrophe is needed.

Correspondence is misspelled.

(4) ***Maybe*** is a lowbrow qualifier; use "might" or "perhaps".

Effect is the noun that describes an influence or outcome. The noun ***affect*** is psychological jargon for "emotion".

(5) The word ***everyday*** means "ordinary"; "every day" means "happening on each day".

The phrase that follows the conjunction ***and*** is not an independent clause (it shares its subject with the clause before the conjunction) so the comma is omitted in this case.

(6) ***Maybe*** is a lowbrow qualifier; use "might" or "perhaps".

Keep the perspective consistent, and try to avoid the use of ***one*** as a pronoun.

Excerpt 3

(1) In surveying their customers and finding that **most** prefer games with lifelike graphics, the computer game company has correctly identified a cause for an increase in the popularity of particular game types. (2) From the evidence presented, it seems reasonable that certain customers buy the more lifelike games in preference to games with inferior graphics. (3) However, the conclusion that game sales will rise as a result of this action neglects to take into account the evidence (4) that the more lifelike games require the latest computer hardware. (5) The argument presents no evidence that the target audience is undergoing a transition to this more advanced, and more expensive, type of computer platform. (6) On the contrary, common sense seems to suggest that, since the target audience tends to be young, that their earning power would not allow them to acquire the equipment necessary to accommodate the games in question, and thus the change in emphasis would not necessarily result in increased sales of those games. (7) If the company were to invest in development of these games, it might waste money in the end.

(1) The company has been ***surveying*** and ***finding***. Changing the verb form to found in the original version violates parallelism and creates confusion.

It's not clear in the original version who ***they*** refers to: it could be the customers or the company. Changing the pronoun clarifies that it is the customers who prefer lifelike games.

(2) Okay is a lowbrow modifier; "reasonable" is more appropriate.

The comma after the introductory clause ***From the evidence presented*** is technically optional, but probably helps prevent possible confusion in this case.

Might maybe is too tentative.

Worse is too lowbrow to be consistent with the tone of the rest of the paragraph; use inferior.

(3) ***End result*** is redundant.

(4) This sentence is a fragment. One easy way to fix the problem is to join this sentence to the previous one. Since it is a restrictive clause (beginning with ***that***) it doesn't need a comma or conjunction—just remove the full stop and the initial capital letter.

New and ***latest*** together are redundant.

(5) Omit the wordy filler phrase ***to show the fact that***

And more expensive is a parenthetic phrase, so it should be followed by a comma.

(6) Add a comma after the introductory phrase ***On the contrary***.

Omit the qualifier ***perhaps*** in this case because, in combination with the verb ***suggests***, it is overly tentative.

Accommodate is misspelled in the original.

The referent of the pronoun ***it*** is unclear in the original version. Specify what ***it*** is with a specific phrase such as ***the change in emphasis*** as shown.

(7) The subjunctive conditional in this sentence takes the "were" form of the verb.

Development is misspelled in the original.

Appendix C: Practice Essay Prompts

Many test takers need most practice in the planning stages of the essay. Once they have begun to develop some ideas for their response, it becomes mere mechanics, but getting started can be a severe stumbling block.

If that's a problem you have (or just worry about) it's a good idea to practise getting started. The following are 22 sample prompts for the essay. Blank space is provided for you to brainstorm and begin to plan your essays.

For additional writing practice, you may also want to type your essay on a computer under timed conditions. Prompts that are marked by an asterisk (*) are those for which sample essays are provided at the end of this section.

Instructions: For each prompt, discuss the extent to which you agree or disagree with the opinion stated, and your reasoning.

Television and radio broadcasts should be closely policed to prevent inappropriate material from airing; this will strengthen the moral fibre of our country.

Individual awards should not be given in youth activities—they lead children to think there can only be one person who deserves praise in any given pursuit.*

Schools should require that students participate in sports to ensure that young adults receive a well-rounded education.

A person can expect to have a successful career if he or she learns how to work in a team environment.

In order to find success, one must learn to balance personal and professional achievement.

The quality of a business can best be judged by looking at the quality of its highest-level managers.

Leaders of democratic countries need to rely on their own best judgment rather than following the will of the people.*

Compromising with one's employees is more effective than demanding results from them.

Recent high-profile corporate scandals point to a desperate need for more ethics classes in business school.

The importance of winning should be de-emphasized in children's sporting activities; only the act of participation should matter.

Any manager who wants improved performance from his or her staff should praise each job well done and should seldom, if ever, criticize a below-par effort.

Our educational system should be structured, from the earliest years, to teach our students how to compete in an increasingly global marketplace.

Government needs to regulate industry to ensure that the environment is protected from companies which will always strive for profits at the expense of the natural world.*

Parents should be held responsible for the actions of their dependent children.

When deciding on a future career, students should consider where their interests lie instead of attempting to maximize their earning ability.

The ultimate goal of a business career should be attaining financial security.

The only music worth listening to is classical music, since it is the only musical genre that has proven its popularity over the course of centuries.

Employees respond best to monetary compensation; no incentive will engender better performance than a raise in salary or a big bonus for a job well done.*

No person acting alone can be as creative or effective in achieving a goal as a team of highly qualified people would be.

People would do better to focus on long-term goals, rather than short-term satisfaction.

The only history that we should teach our children is our own country's history. This will boost their patriotism.*

Some parents believe their children should receive as broad an education as possible; but children would be better served by studies that prepare them for a specific career.

SAMPLE ESSAYS

Here are sample essays for five of the sample prompts. Remember that an essay does not have to be perfect. Review these essays and note which qualities make them exemplary.

"Individual awards should not be given in youth activities—they lead children to think there can only be one person who deserves praise in any given pursuit."

While it should not be the aim of youth activities to promote hyper-competition between children, it does not follow that individual awards should not be used. In fact, individual awards have the benefit of teaching valuable lessons to children. Through the bestowal of individual honours, children will learn that notable efforts deserve praise, they will see role models in their peers in terms of how to perform, and they will also gain knowledge of how our competitive world works.

The first major benefit of individual awards in youth activities is that it teaches children that there are rewards for stellar efforts. Pavlov showed decades ago the power of positive reinforcement and everything from dog training to child psychology has adopted its tenets. If there is a positive prize, such as an individual award, children will learn to strive for better results, whether the activity is youth football or other activity. My eleven year-old niece has developed into a fine poet primarily because of the praise and awards she received in poetry exercises as a grammar school student.

Another positive factor associated with individual awards in youth sports is that children will gain necessary role models in their peer group. A child who dreams of being a star basketball player can always look to the professional leagues and model themselves after Vince Carter or Tim Duncan. However, young children cannot possibly mimic the behaviour of these international stars on the court. A child would be much better off trying to compete with the acknowledged star of the youth league. When I was a young swimmer, I did not ever try to train to compete with the Olympic athletes. I simply tried to become the best on my team, then the best in my league, and so on. I benefited from watching the work ethic and strokes of the awarded athletes around me, not the stars that I could not possibly compare myself to.

The final benefit of individual awards is that it teaches children that we live in a competitive world. There is no reason that teachers, parents, and coaches should teach their children to cheat to get ahead. However, children must learn that there is a competitive world waiting on the other side of childhood where better performers are more successful.

Skeptics of this viewpoint might disparage these arguments by stating that children do learn to be cut-throat from individual awards or that individual awards kill a sense of team play. Even individual awards can be structured in such a way that these concerns will be addressed. First of all, awards can be given in a variety of activities so that the individual talent of every participant is recognized. Young Jim may be the best basketball player, but Timmy can win for best acting skills. Second, multiple awards can be given for the same activity. Again, this will emphasize that everyone is good at something. Tina might win for best football defence while Alexis wins for best shooting. Finally, awards can be given for best spirit or best team player. Recognizing the ability to sacrifice for the common good and be a team player will encourage this activity in the future lives of youths.

While individual awards may spawn competition between children, they can be structured to prevent children from becoming overly focused on competition. Individual awards have a number of important benefits. Among these benefits are the behavioural effects of positive reinforcement, the granting of young role models, and the lessons provided in the way that the "real" world works.

"Leaders of democratic countries need to rely on their own best judgment rather than following the will of the people."

In representative democracies, voters select leaders to make decisions. This is in contrast to direct democracy, where voters make decisions directly. Although there are isolated examples of direct democracy, in local Swiss government, in referendums, and in petitions for change, direct democracy is difficult to practise, and elected representatives make most decisions in most democratic nations. In representative democracy, leaders must rely on their best judgment and not always follow the "will of the people." Not only are leaders selected for this very role, but also they typically have more information upon which to make decisions, and more time to weigh the issues than do voters. Also, judging the "will of the people" is difficult.

Two advantages that elected leaders have over voting citizens are greater quantities of information and time. For example, the office of the President of the United States receives information from many parts of the executive branch, and has hundreds of researchers collecting and distilling information. Few voters would have the time or the expertise to distill and make use of such information. In addition, the President has a job where he or she is afforded the time to make important decisions, and where he or she must make decisions constantly. It would be impractical to expect American voters to similarly devote large portions of their time to ponder questions of foreign trade or domestic policy, and to make quick, important decisions when such decisions must be made.

A final reason that leaders should act on their own judgment is the difficulty in precisely determining public opinion. Much of the work in determining public opinion is currently done through polling small "representative" samples of the public. Polls, however, can be skewed by many factors including how a question is asked, and what time of day the poll administrator calls. Also, many respondents are unsure of their answers, and seek merely to please the administrators. When groups of individuals are placed in groups to discuss policies, or when respondents are presented with certain facts, the results can vary dramatically from poll results. Opinion poll results are also known to contradict each other, to move wildly in a short period of time, and, sometimes, to be inaccurate. On many issues, it would be very difficult to assess public opinion with a high degree of accuracy.

An elected leader has an obligation to act according to his or her best interest because he or she has more information, more time, and a defined role tailored for making decisions for the people. In addition, a leader has little chance of knowing the "true" will of the people at every moment because of the logistical difficult es inherent in measuring the opinions of people.

"Government needs to regulate industry to ensure that the environment is protected from companies which will always strive for profits at the expense of the natural world."

It may not be true that companies will "always" strive for profits at the expense of the environment; however, government authorities should take an active role in policing the actions of corporate entities to ensure that commitment to the profit motive does not have deleterious effects on our environment. Some companies do show a serious concern for the natural world, but even a few transgressors can cause significant harm to the ecosystem. Regulators must lay down the primary line of defence in protecting the environment, making sure that a series of small offences do not combine to have a major impact.

The primary concern of companies is to increase their profits and therefore the value of the enterprise. Because of this, companies are given a strong incentive to slash costs wherever possible. Examples may include putting run-off from a factory directly into a stream, river, or ocean without treating it first or allowing smoke from a coal burning power plant to flow unhindered into the atmosphere. Building treatment facilities or installing smoke stack scrubbers are almost never in the best interests of individual companies. Since companies do not face the costs of polluting streams or the atmosphere, they will increase profits by polluting.

In fact, some of the worst pollution industries have never voluntarily taken pollution control measures. Before recent legislation and enforcement that requires the use of smoke stack scrubbers in coal burning power plants, all the coal plants in the United States were letting SOx and NOx gasses flow directly into the atmosphere. Similarly, the mining industry never treated mine runoff before environmental regulations required them to do so. The oil refining industry is another that has had to make considerable changes against its will to improve its environmental track record.

Some may argue that the past thirty years or so have seen more and more companies displaying a "green," or ecologically informed, sensibility in their decision-making and that therefore government regulation is no longer needed. This development, however, should not lull government leaders into a reduced degree of vigilance. Even if the majority of business concerns were environmentally responsible, it would only take one company's negligence to bring about an ecological disaster. Most of the environmental tragedies of the last few decades—for example, Love Canal, the Exxon Valdez, and the real-life events depicted in "Erin Brockovich"—have been attributable to individual corporations.

Even businesses that one might characterize as "environmentally aware" may choose to skirt environmental regulations by incremental degrees in the pursuit of greater profitability. If every company, however, were to sanction such small infractions, the collective effect could be considerable.

While it is not true that companies will always sacrifice the environment for increased profits, it is definitely true that government needs to regulate industry to protect the natural world. Without regulation, too many companies would be tempted by profits to slash the costs required for environmental clean-up or would never see a reason to improve their current polluting operations. Government watchfulness in matters of environmental protection will provide the requisite insurance against all manifestations of ecological disregard, from the single catastrophic event to the stealthy accumulation of cut corners.

"Employees respond best to monetary compensation; no incentive will engender better performance than a raise in salary or a big bonus for a job well done."

While compensation plays an important role in encouraging optimal employee performance, money is not the most effective incentive. Money works more at the foundational level of motivation, convincing an employee to accept a job. Other, less tangible methods must be employed to engender peak performance once the employee is at work. These methods may range from public praise for a job well done to greater degrees of decision-making power.

Less straightforward rewards can be very effective in fostering exemplary performance. Many firms, for example, reward high-performing executives with the option to buy shares of the company's stock at prices lower than the normal trading range of the stock. While money is still involved, the long-term aspect of this reward encourages a similarly long-term commitment to the employer, and a focus on years to come rather than on next week's pay cheque.

Many other types of incentives have no financial element. Simple words of praise delivered consistently and, when warranted, before the employee's peer group, can do much to win a subordinate's commitment to a higher level of performance. When I began my first job at a consulting firm after university, my manager got the most out of me by praising a job well done. I was always highly motivated to again earn her praise.

Promotions can also have positive effects, as long as the promotion is truly one of responsibility and not in title alone. Many motivated people dream of making decisions for themselves at work and often wish to have their "boss's job". When a person gets a true promotion, they often feel that added responsibility deserves added efforts and put even more of themselves into their work.

Finally, employees can also be motivated through inspirational leadership. Those that pour their hearts out for a political campaign are rarely doing so because of the financial rewards that they might reap. In fact, many volunteer their time and tireless efforts with no expectation of financial reward. They work so hard because they believe in the positive effect that their candidate or policy might have, if elected or enacted. This same motivation can also work in a company. Employees will often respond well to a hard-working, fair, and dedicated manager.

None of this is to say that money does not play a role in motivation. However, monetary compensation serves as what the eminent twentieth century motivational expert Frederick Herzberg termed a "dissatisfier". According to Herzberg, if an employee perceived himself or herself to be underpaid, that perception worked to increase dissatisfaction and strongly reduce the motivation to perform. Conversely, if the employee perceived himself or herself to be compensated fairly or overpaid this might have engendered some sense of personal satisfaction or comfort, but it wouldn't have necessarily translated into outstanding job performance. The perception of insufficient compensation can dissatisfy an employee, but the perception of sufficient compensation is not a great driver to higher performance. On some level, the employee may feel naturally entitled to the higher rate of pay.

While it is true that remuneration is a necessary ingredient in employee motivation, it is not sufficient. Most people enjoy the sense of belonging to a winning team and of contributing to a worthy endeavour. They also may respond well to praise or increases in responsibility. Still other incentives involve longer-term financial compensation without a raise in salary or a big bonus.

"The only history that we should teach our children is our own country's history; this will boost their patriotism."

The author of this opinion would have readers believe that schools in this country should only teach English history to students because this will increase their patriotism. There are, however, many negative effects of teaching only a unilateral view of history, including the inability to learn from the mistakes and successes of others, the lack of understanding of other cultures, and the feeling of over-importance that children may derive. It also remains unclear if teaching only English history would actually have the salubrious effect of increasing patriotism. Therefore, I do not agree with the opinion expressed above.

The first negative effect of teaching only our own history is that it does not let our children, who are the future leaders of this country, learn from the mistakes of others. The study of history allows young people to see how difficult situations were handled in the past. Students might learn the success of negotiated peace from Anwar Sadat and Menachem Begin by studying foreign histories. If students studied only our history, they would miss out on many of these valuable lessons.

The second ill-effect is that studying only our history does not allow students to gain an appreciation and understanding of foreign cultures. In this increasingly global marketplace in which we live, it is critical that our political and business leaders of tomorrow understand their counterparts in other nations. Without studying global history, our future leaders would not understand the critical and delicate situations in North Korea or the Middle East. If our leaders do not understand the background to these situations, there could be disastrous effects. It would also be very important for business leaders to understand the culture and history of the markets into which they hope to sell our goods.

The final negative factor is that our children might become overly intrepid if they believe that the only history worth noting is English history. Not only would our future political leaders not have an understanding of their counterparties as discussed above, but also they may develop into overbearing and unilateral negotiators. The situation of North Korea outlined above could be greatly compounded if our future leaders did not understand the situation, and as a result attempted to bully the North Koreans into acting a certain way. Similarly, our future business leaders would not be as effective if they tried to control partners in other nations.

Some might argue that the patriotic benefits derived from teaching only our history would outweigh the negatives. While I do not believe this would be the case even if the patriotic benefits were significant, I further believe that the benefits would not materialize. If our schools taught only our history, but taught it in a balanced and fair manner, there would be much for our young people to regret about the actions of our predecessors. This might actually hamper patriotism. For example, the English are responsible for hundreds of years of slavery in its colonies, for the massacre of indigenous peoples, for a bloody civil war and for supporting totalitarian administrations in other nations. While our history is full of laudable accomplishments, if it is taught in a balance manner, our students would not necessarily be more patriotic.

It does not make sense to teach our children only the history of this nation. There could be several negative effects, including the loss of important examples, of cultural understanding, and of proper decorum. In addition, the opinion that the main benefit of teaching only our history is increased patriotism is unsubstantiated.

Notes

Notes

Notes

Notes

Notes

Notes

Notes

Notes